SKILL SHARPENERS
Critical Thinking
Grade 3

The following illustrations were created by the artists listed (provided through Shutterstock.com) and are protected by copyright: bluedog studio, DibaniMedia, Edwin Butter, olga_gl (page 8); Teguh Mujiono (page 9); Vidoslava (pages 9, 21); GraphicsRF (pages 10, 16, 74, 75, 77, 89, 94, 95, 97, 99, 128, 129); totallyjamie (page 11); Alexander Kazantsev, Farhad Bek (page 12); Kjersti Joergensen (page 14); Marchenko Olga, MatoomMi (page 15); subarashii21 (pages 17, 93); Monkik, Sarawut Padungkwan (page 18); victoria pineapple (pages 20, 21, 22); XiXStockPhotos (page 24); Lorelyn Medina (pages 25, 41, 44, 95, 96); tikiri (page 26); Monticello, Pop Paul-Catalin (page 28); Neonic Flower (page 29); Loradora, Tatiana Kuzmina (page 30); K N (page 31); vectorOK (page 32); Kelvin Wong, PCHT, Phovoir (page 33); daisybee (page 35); Bokeh Blur Background Subject, Mariyana M, MyImages – Micha, sevenke, Valeri Potapova, Vitaly Zorkin, Yellow Cat (page 40); Billion Photos, jocic, Mathee saengkaew, pirtuss, Scanrail1 (page 41); yurgo (pages 41, 48); Iulian Dragomir (page 42); ollomy (page 44); Picsfive, Robert Babczynski (page 45); AlenKadr, BW Folsom, Levent Konuk, Svetlana Foote, You Touch Pix of EuToch (page 49); mama_mia (page 51); AlohaHawaii, gorillaimages, Hurst Photo, Rawpixel.com (page 56); Tomacco (page 57); Gajus, hoyou (page 58); Skokan Olena (page 60); Pushkin (page 61); Transia Design (page 62); Alex Staroseltsev, ayelet-keshet, Eric Isselee, fantom_rd, MilsiArt, Peter Wollinga, Sarycheva Olesia (page 63); Bonezboyz (page 65); Joana Lopes (page 72); Monkey Business Images (pages 72, 88, 120); jenjira, Vector (page 74); Tatiana Gulyaeva (page 78); lukpedclub, SlipFloat (page 80); mcherevan (page 81); Anna.zabella, Elvetica (page 82); Victor Brave (pages 82, 91); Iconic Bestiary (page 83); sasimoto (page 85); PedroMatos (page 88); Laia Design Studio, StepanPopov (page 89); Cory Thoman (page 90); D.J.McGee, kak2s, tovovan (page 92); Virinaflora (page 97); pockygallery (page 98); candycatdesigns, pingvin_house (page 104); Jane Kelly, Kit8.net, Red monkey (page 105); alazur (page 106); Dmitry Natashin (pages 106, 115); Mallinka1, Sunny Kate (page 107); SVStudio (page 108); Danny Xu (page 110); RJC Cartoons (pages 111, 131); petovarga (page 112); notkoo (page 113); Fleren (page 114); kiberstalker (page 117); bilha Golan, Sergey Chirkov (page 120); Beresnev (page 121); zsooofija (pages 121, 125); kikoo (pages 121, 127); infoland, Photoexpert (page 122); AboliC, arbit (page 123); E. Druzhinina, Yayayoyo (page 124); Incomible (page 126); artbesouro, DVARG, Liliya Shlapak, Macrovector, Spreadthesign (page 129)

Editorial Development: Rachel Lynette
Jo Ellen Moore
Lisa Vitarisi Mathews
Copy Editing: Cindie Farley
Art Direction: Yuki Meyer
Design/Production: Cheryl Puckett
Yuki Meyer
Jessica Onken

EMC 3253

Helping Children Learn

Visit
teaching-standards.com
to view a correlation
of this book.
This is a free service.

**Correlated to
Current Standards**

**Congratulations on your purchase of some of the
finest teaching materials in the world.**

CPSIA: Asia Pacific Offset Ltd, Kowloon, Hong Kong [10/2020]

Contents

Places

Our World

How to Use This Book

Practicing Critical Thinking Skills

Critical thinking comes naturally to young children. They learn autonomy through exploration, observe their environment using logic and reasoning, try new things, and think creatively. As children grow and enter an academic setting, some of their natural curiosity and problem-solving instincts are not engaged as often as they could be. This practice book encourages children to "think about their thinking" through creative, analytical, and evaluative tasks.

Read All About It

Read the selection to your child. Discuss how the illustrations help your child better understand the topic. Then, if your child is able, have him or her read the selection to you. After reading the selection, discuss how the topic relates to your child's life.

Tell What You Know

The activities on these pages provide opportunities for children to connect their knowledge and opinions to the topic. Encourage your child to think about his or her experiences and support his or her curiosity by discussing the questions and topics together.

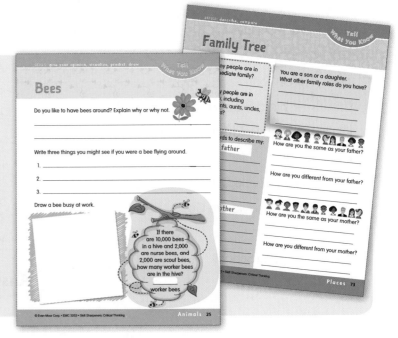

Critical Thinking Activities

The critical thinking activities are designed to engage children in application, analytical, and evaluative tasks. The cross-curricular activities present science, math, social studies, and language arts content.

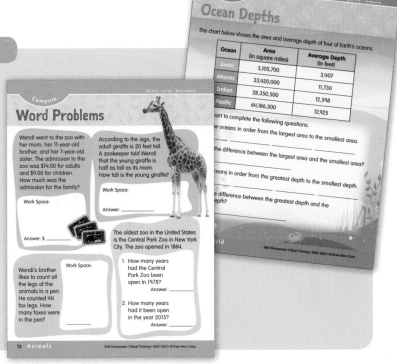

Art Projects and Hands-on Activities

The art projects and hands-on activities provide children with opportunities to use critical thinking skills to create. Encourage your child to tap into his or her creativity and innovation and to have fun with the hands-on activities. After your child completes each project, discuss the steps taken to create it. Encourage your child to explain what he or she enjoyed most and why.

6

Monkeys

✓ I Did It! Check each activity as you complete it.

Be on the Lookout!

How many times can you find the word **monkey** on pages 9–11? Count and write the number here: _____

Facts About Monkeys

Read about monkeys, then answer the questions on the following pages.

Whoop! Whoop! Whoop! What is that loud sound? It's the call of the howler monkey. The loud call can be heard from as far as three miles away. The howler is one of about 250 different kinds of monkeys living in the forests, in the mountains, and on the grasslands around the world.

Monkeys have large brains, long tails, hands, eyes that look forward, and feet that can grasp tree branches. Most New World monkeys (those that live in Central and South America) have prehensile tails. This means their tails can be used to hang on to tree branches. Most Old World monkeys (those that live in Africa and Asia) have tails, but they are not prehensile.

Monkeys come in many sizes and shapes. The smallest monkey is the pygmy marmoset. It is about five inches long and weighs about four ounces. The largest monkey is the male mandrill. It is over three feet tall and weighs about 75 pounds.

Most monkeys eat plant parts such as nuts, fruits, seeds, flowers, and leaves. They also eat animals such as insects, spiders, and birds' eggs. Those living near water also hunt for crabs, clams, and small water animals. Some monkeys use large branches to kill food, such as snakes. Capuchin monkeys even use tools to get their food. They smash nuts with rocks. They poke small twigs or branches into holes to pull out insects.

Monkeys are social creatures. They live in groups called troops. The troop works together to care for their young and to protect one another. The strongest male in the troop is the leader.

Think about what you have learned about monkeys. What is one way New World monkeys and Old World monkeys are alike? How are they different?

Monkeys

How would you describe a monkey to someone who has never seen one?

<u>Brown and tan animals that</u>

<u>eax ~~ten~~ ~~bear~~ ~~bena~~</u>

<u>bananas.</u>

Use the letters in **MONKEYS** to make a word for each clue.

used to unlock _____

dollars and cents _____

opposite of no _____

before two _____

comes from fire _____

Each monkey at the zoo eats 6 bananas every day. There are 7 monkeys. How many bananas will be needed for…

1 day? _____

2 days? _____

4 days? _____

1 week? _____

Write this sentence correctly.

Matt saw 7 monkies at the zoo.

_____

Compare

Think About It

How are monkeys the same as humans? How are they different?
Fill in the chart with 3 ways for each.

Same	Different

Jane went to Africa to see monkeys.
She saw 3 fewer monkeys on the
second day than she did on the first day.
She saw 6 monkeys on the third day.
She saw twice as many monkeys on
the first day as she did on the third day.
How many monkeys did Jane see
on each day? How many
did she see in all?

First day: _____

Second day: _____

Third day: _____

In all: _____

What is this?

_____

_____

_____

Skill Sharpeners: Critical Thinking • EMC 3253 • © Evan-Moor Corp.

Animal Idioms

Fill in the blank with the name of an animal from the box to complete each idiom.

Word Box	
fly	ants
bat	goose
cat	bird
horse	camel
frog	monkeys
worms	mouse

1. _____ in your pants

2. _____ in my throat

3. as blind as a _____

4. Has the _____ got your tongue?

5. wouldn't hurt a _____

6. so hungry, I could eat a _____

7. more fun than a barrel of _____

8. as quiet as a _____

9. a can of _____

10. a _____'s-eye view

11. go on a wild _____ chase

12. the straw that broke the _____'s back

Compute

Word Problems

Wendi went to the zoo with her mom, her 11-year-old brother, and her 7-year-old sister. The admission to the zoo was $14.00 for adults and $9.00 for children. How much was the admission for the family?

Work Space:

Answer: $ _____

According to the sign, the adult giraffe is 20 feet tall. A zookeeper told Wendi that the young giraffe is half as tall as its mom. How tall is the young giraffe?

Work Space:

Answer: _____

The oldest zoo in the United States is the Central Park Zoo in New York City. The zoo opened in 1864.

Wendi's brother likes to count all the legs of the animals in a pen. He counted 44 fox legs. How many foxes were in the pen?

Work Space:

_____

1. How many years had the Central Park Zoo been open in 1978?

   Answer: _____

2. How many years had it been open in the year 2015?

   Answer: _____

Skill Sharpeners: Critical Thinking • EMC 3253 • © Evan-Moor Corp.

Make a Monkey

Follow the directions to draw a monkey.
Then color your monkey and fill in the blanks.

This monkey lives in the _____.

It uses its _____ and _____ to move in trees.

A monkey can _____.

...nkey Words

Monkey begins with **MON**. Each of the answers to the clues also contains **MON**. Use the clues to complete the words. If a letter has a number below it, write that letter at the bottom of the page to find the kind of monkey that you see.

expensive gem	___ ___ ___ **MON** ___ 3
popular board game	**MON** ___ ___ ___ ___ 2 8 12
rare or unusual	___ ___ ___ ___ **MON** 9 7
scary creature	**MON** ___ ___ ___ ___ 6
12 in a year	**MON** ___ ___ ___ 1
type of nut	___ ___ **MON** ___ 4
Japanese robe	___ **MON** ___ 10
coins and bills	**MON** ___ ___ 5
yellow fruit	___ ___ **MON** 11

___ ___ ___ ___ ___ ___   ___ ___ ___ ___ ___ ___
1   2   3   4   5   6   7   8   9   10   11   12

    Skill Sharpeners: Critical Thinking • EMC 3253 • © Evan-Moor Corp.

Monkey Snack

Complete the paragraph.

Monkey Snack

Last week at the zoo, I saw a monkey eat a banana. This is what it did.

First, _____

Then, _____

Finally, it _____

_____

_____

Maybe I'll eat one myself!

Pretend you are going to eat an orange. Write a topic sentence. Give at least three steps telling what you will do.

_____

_____

_____

_____

Generate

Word Chains

To make a word chain, each word must begin with the same letter that the last word ends with. Finish the word chain for each category.

Example: <u>Animals</u>

monke**y**

ya**k**

kangaro**o**

ostrich

Kinds of Foods	Places	Animals
pizza	Orego**n**	wolf
asparagus	**N**ew York	**f**lamingo

Skill Sharpeners: Critical Thinking • EMC 3253 • © Evan-Moor Corp.

It's Feeding Time!

Tyson enjoys watching the zookeepers feed the animals. The feeding schedule for some of the zoo animals is given below. Design a schedule for Tyson so that he can see as many animals being fed as possible.

Remember:

- He wants to see each animal being fed for the full time.
- He can <u>not</u> see more than one animal at a time.

Penguins	9:00 to 9:30 a.m.
Seals	9:15 to 9:30 a.m.
Tigers	10:00 to 10:30 a.m.
Lions	10:00 to 10:30 a.m.
Bears	10:30 to 10:45 a.m.
Hippos	10:30 to 11:00 a.m.
Elephants	10:45 to 11:00 a.m.
Monkeys	11:00 to 11:30 a.m.
Apes	11:00 to 11:15 a.m.
Anteaters	11:15 to 11:30 a.m.

_____

_____

_____

Create

Monkey Paper Chains

What You Do:

1. Remove page 19 from the book. Color the monkeys.

2. Cut the two patterns apart.

3. Carefully fold one of the monkey patterns like an accordion, along the black lines. The monkey must be on top of the folded paper.

4. Cut out the yellow shaded sections.

5. Open the paper to see a row of monkeys.

6. Follow the same steps to make the other monkey chain.

7. Refold the two chains. Glue them to page 21.

Skill Sharpeners: Critical Thinking • EMC 3253 • © Evan-Moor Corp.

Glue one
monkey chain
here

Glue one
monkey chain
here

I know three interesting facts about monkeys:

1. _____

_____

2. _____

_____

3. _____

_____

Bees

✓ I Did It! Check each activity as you complete it.

Be on the Lookout!

How many different **bees** can you find on pages 24–34?
Count them and write the number here: _____

Facts About Bees

Read about bees, then answer the questions on the following pages.

You might think that there is only one type of bee, the kind that buzzes around your food when you eat outside. But, there are many, many types of bees. In fact, there are about 20,000 species of bees around the world. But all bees are alike in these ways:

- three body parts
- six legs
- two pairs of wings

- antennae
- compound eyes and simple eyes

Let's learn more about the hardworking bees who make honey—the honeybees! Honeybees are helpful to people in many ways. Besides making honey, they make beeswax. They also pollinate plants. As they gather the nectar from flowers, pollen sticks to their bodies. When they land on a new flower, some of the pollen falls off. This helps the flower make seeds for new plants.

Honeybees are social insects. They live in groups in a hive. Each honeybee has a job to do. The queen lays eggs. Drones mate with the queen so she can make the eggs. Worker bees do all of the work. They build the hive out of beeswax. They clean and protect the hive. They gather nectar to make honey for food. Most of the bees in a hive are worker bees.

Here are other interesting facts about honeybees:
1. The buzzing sound made by bees is made when they flap their wings.
2. Honeybees can fly up to six miles.
3. If a honeybee stings someone, it will die.
4. Honeybees use the sun as a compass to guide their flight.
5. They dance to share information with other honeybees.

Bees

Do you like to have bees around? Explain why or why not.

_____

_____

Write three things you might see if you were a bee flying around.

1. _____

2. _____

3. _____

Draw a bee busy at work.

If there are 10,000 bees in a hive and 2,000 are nurse bees, and 2,000 are scout bees, how many worker bees are in the hive?

_____

worker bees

Analyze

Bzzzzzzzz

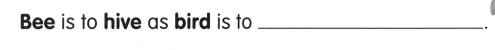

Bee is to **hive** as **bird** is to _____.

Bee is to **sting** as **mosquito** is to _____.

Bee is to **yellow** as **polar bear** is to _____.

Bees can sting. What are 3 other animals that can sting?

1. _____   2. _____   3. _____

Bees have stripes. What are 3 other animals that have stripes?

1. _____   2. _____   3. _____

Betty Bee is an odd bee. She will gather nectar <u>only</u> from the flowers with odd-numbered products. Color those flowers.

Why Not?

Circle the picture or word in each line that does <u>not</u> share the same attributes as others in the line.

1. bee   spider   fly   wasp   gnat

Why? _____

2. cake   pie   cookie   donut   pretzel

Why? _____

3.

Why? _____

4. daffodil   tulip   daisy   pine   rose

Why? _____

5.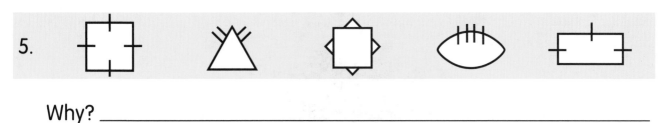

Why? _____

Compute

Word Problems

Minna loves stuffed animals. Bees are her favorite. She displays her stuffed-animal collection in 2 cabinets. In one cabinet, there are 8 large animals on each shelf. In the other cabinet, there are 9 small animals on each shelf. If each cabinet has 7 shelves, how many large and small animals are in each cabinet? How many animals are in both cabinets?

Work Space:

_____ large animals

_____ small animals

_____ animals in all

Last year Minna bought 3 stuffed animals for $4.50 each, 2 stuffed animals for $5.00 each, and 1 for $5.50. How much did she spend on stuffed animals last year?

Work Space:

$_____

Minna has a book that tells how much the stuffed animals are worth. Buzzy Bee first sold for $4.50. It was worth 40¢ more each month for the next 6 months. How much is it worth now?

Work Space:

$_____

Skill Sharpeners: Critical Thinking • EMC 3253 • © Evan-Moor Corp.

Be Ready!

A bee is buzzing near you and it won't go away. What should you do? Rate these ideas from 1 to 6. The best idea should be number 1.

_____ Run away.

_____ Stand as still as possible.

_____ Scream.

_____ Ignore it.

_____ Sing it a song.

_____ Swat it.

Complete the words that begin with **be**.

Look out be_____!

Be_____ of the dog.

Be_____ in yourself.

He was be_____ himself.

To infinity and be_____!

Just be_____ you and me…

Be_____ I said so!

Look be_____ you leap.

Write 3 kinds of sentences about bees.

Boring: _____

Interesting: _____

Silly: _____

Distinguish

It's a Bee!

Read about the parts of a worker bee.

- Her long **tongue** works like a straw. She uses it to sip nectar from flowers.

- She feels and smells with two **antennae** on her head.

- She has four **wings** that are used for flying.

- She crawls and climbs about on her six **legs**.

- She has three body parts—a **head** in front, a **thorax** in the middle, and an **abdomen** in back.

- She uses a **stinger** at the end of her abdomen to defend herself.

Label the parts of this bee.

Skill Sharpeners: Critical Thinking • EMC 3253 • © Evan-Moor Corp.

A New Insect

You just discovered a new kind of insect! Answer the questions about your insect. Then draw a picture of your insect on the leaf.

1. What is your insect's name?

   _____

   _____

2. What size and shape is your insect?

   _____

   _____

3. What color is your insect?

   _____

   _____

4. Where does your insect live?

   _____

   _____

5. How does your insect get around?

   _____

   _____

6. What is special about your insect?

   _____

   _____

Compose

A Bee Cinquain

Follow the steps to write a cinquain about bees.

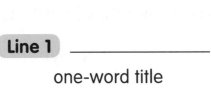

Line 1 _____

one-word title

Line 2 _____ _____

two words about the title

Line 3 _____ _____ _____

three words describing an action

Line 4 _____ _____ _____ _____

four words describing a feeling

Line 5 _____

one-word synonym for the title (or repeat the title)

Now illustrate your poem.

What's Important?

In each situation below, decide which details are relevant.
Circle **all** the relevant details for each situation.

1. You are near a beehive.

- what you are eating
- if you disturb the hive
- if it is windy
- what you are wearing
- what you are drinking

2. You are making a cake.

- the temperature of the oven
- who likes cake
- what ingredients you need
- how long the cake needs to bake
- who gets the first piece

3. You are having a test in social studies.

- what the test is about
- the number of questions on the test
- what type of test it will be
- your score on the last test
- when the test is scheduled

Now try these on your own.

4. What details are **relevant** to buying your mother a birthday present?

_____

5. What details are **irrelevant** to choosing a best friend?

_____

Infer

A Honeybee's Body

Write the name of each body part of the honeybee's body on the correct line.

Word Box

antenna   leg   head   eye

pollen basket   tongue   stinger   wing

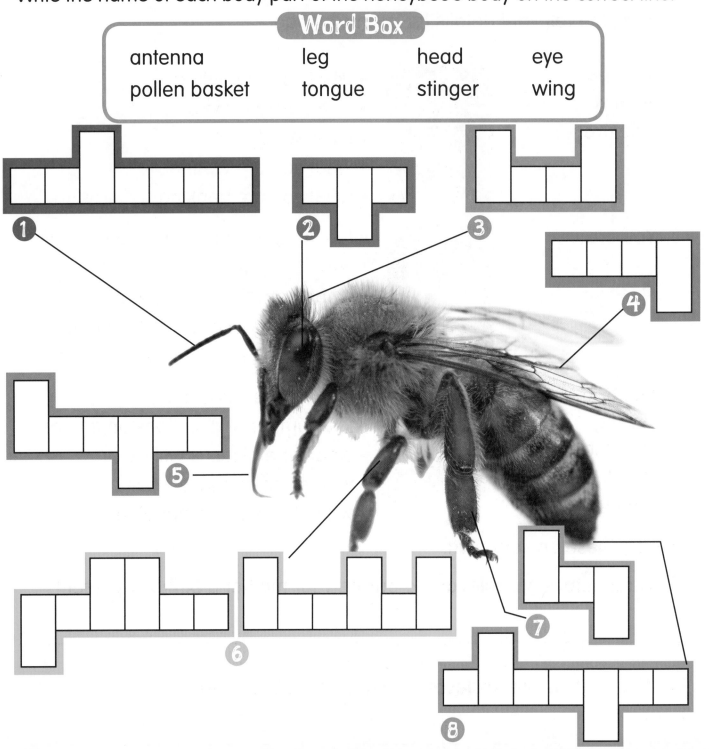

Solve

Flower to Flower

Bonnie Bee is gathering letters instead of nectar! Read the clues to find the letters she gathered. Write the letters in order on the lines below to solve the riddle.

- top-right corner

- just to the right of **Z**

- two flowers down from **G**

- just above **A**

- down and to the left of **T**

- bottom center

- up and to the left of **X**

- down and to the left of **L**

- down and to the left of **Q**

What kind of gum does a bee chew?

___ ___ ___   ___ ___ ___   ___ ___ ___!

Create

Bee Origami

What You Need:

- page 37
- tape
- scissors

Follow the dotted line to cut out the large square on page 37.

1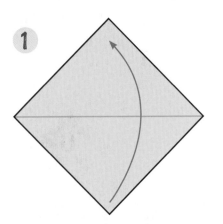

2

Fold the right corner to the top corner.

3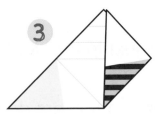

4

Fold the left corner to the top corner.

5

Fold down.

6

7

Fold over on first line.

8

Fold over on next line.

9

Fold over one more time.

10

Fold back and tape.

11

"It's a bee!"

Skill Sharpeners: Critical Thinking • EMC 3253 • © Evan-Moor Corp.

Skill Sharpeners: Critical Thinking • EMC 3253 • © Evan-Moor Corp.

Things We Use

✓ I Did It! Check each activity as you complete it.

Be on the Lookout!

How many times can you find the word **use** on pages 41–46? Count and write the number here: _____

Facts About Things We Use

Read about things we use, then answer the questions on the following pages.

Think about how many different things we use in our everyday lives. We use pencils, paper, computers, locks, keys, bottles, and jars—and the list goes on and on!

Do you ever wonder who invented the things you use? Or when they were invented? Or why they were invented? Most things are invented because of a need.

✓ People needed a writing tool that they could carry with them.

✓ People needed to keep their things safe.

✓ People needed a way to keep food fresh and sealed tightly.

Some of the things we use are tools that help make jobs in our everyday lives easier. For example, a computer is a tool. A key is a tool. A pencil is a tool. Tools are used at home, at school, at work, and at many other places such as restaurants and hospitals. What tools do you use at home? What tools do you use at school? Do your parents use tools to do their jobs?

We use some things so often that we may not know what to do without them. Many people use computers every day. They send email, shop online, watch shows, and write papers. Some people use bottles and jars to hold their foods, spices, nails and screws, and office supplies. Look around your house and notice containers like bottles and jars that help keep things fresh. Look around and see if you are also using the bottles or jars to keep things tidy and organized. What would we do if we didn't have all of the things we use every day?

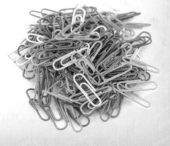

Skill Sharpeners: Critical Thinking • EMC 3253 • © Evan-Moor Corp.

I Use These!

Write to tell how you use each thing.

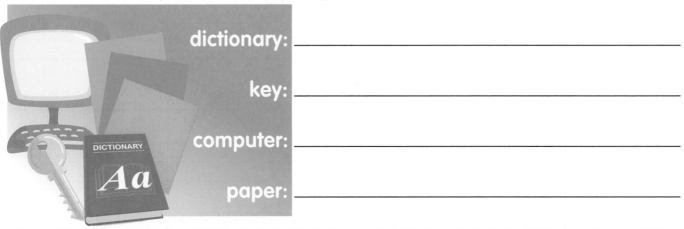

dictionary: _____

key: _____

computer: _____

paper: _____

Put these things into two groups. Write the names in the boxes.
Tell someone about the groups you made.

Group 1

Group 2

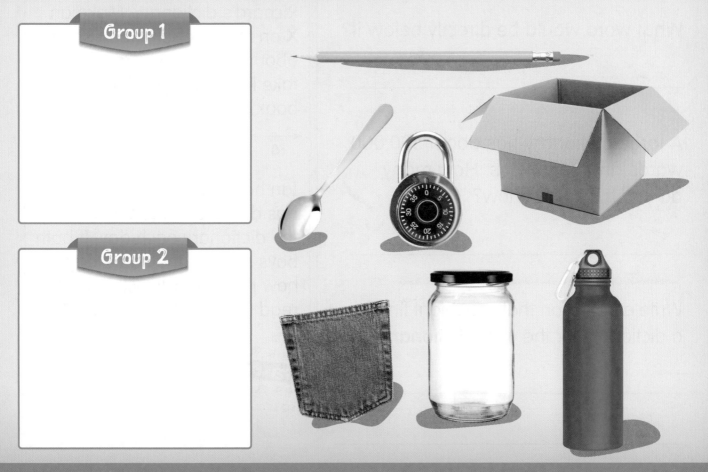

Suggest

We Use a Dictionary

What are 3 things you could use a dictionary for?

1. _____

2. _____

3. _____

If your name were in the dictionary, what word would be directly above it?

_____

What word would be directly below it?

_____

A large dictionary has about 500,000 words and definitions. How many do you think you know?

_____

Write a definition that you might find in a dictionary for the word **dictionary**.

_____

_____

Richard has decided to read the entire dictionary. His plan is to read one page each day. There are 1,825 pages in Richard's dictionary. Make an **X** on the number line to show about how many years it will take Richard to read the entire book.

0 1 2 3 4 5 6 7 8

Ian has a different plan. He has decided to read 3 words in the dictionary each day. If both boys start on the same day, how many words will Ian have read when Richard is done?

_____ words

We Use Locks and Keys

What are 10 things that you might need to open with a key?

1. _____

2. _____

3. _____

4. _____

5. _____

6. _____

7. _____

8. _____

9. _____

10. _____

Use the clues to find the words. Each word rhymes with either **LOCK** or **KEY**.

has a trunk _____

stone _____

to speak _____

look _____

part of leg _____

on your foot _____

hot drink _____

tells the time _____

group of sheep _____

not a prisoner _____

Shelby has a combination lock for her bike. Use the clues to find her combination.

- The combination is a 3-digit number.

- The first and third digits are even.

- The middle digit is 3 more than the last digit.

- The middle digit is 7 more than the first digit.

- If you add all the digits together, you get 17.

What is Shelby's combination? _____

Specify

We Use Computers

What do people use computers for?

1. _____   5. _____

2. _____   6. _____

3. _____   7. _____

4. _____   8. _____

Most American children watch about 3 hours of television every day. How many hours of TV is that in a week?

_____ hours in a week

About how many hours of TV do you watch…

in a day? _____

in a week? _____

What does this say?

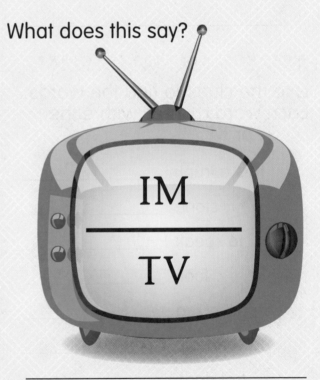

IM
___
TV

_____

Do you think you watch too much TV? _____

Why or why not? _____

We Use Pencils

Which do you like better—traditional wooden pencils or mechanical pencils?

_____ Why? _____

_____

What materials were used to make your pencil?

_____

_____

_____

_____

Try to balance your pencil on your finger for 10 seconds.

Could you do it?

☐ **yes**   ☐ **no**

Draw a realistic picture of your pencil.

Besides writing and erasing, what are some other things that you can do with a pencil?

1._____

2._____

3._____

4._____

5._____

6._____

How many pencils are in your desk right now?

Guess: _____   Actual number: _____

Plan

We Use Paper

You need to write down a phone number, but you don't have any paper. What can you use instead?

_____

The word **paper** begins with **p** and ends in **r**. Use the clues to make other words that begin with **p** and end in **r**.

a fruit   p_____r

game participant   p_____r

not rich   p_____r

two of a kind   p_____r

The yellow paper is under the red paper. The blue paper is on the top. The green paper is between the blue and red papers. Color the papers.

Draw lines to show how you could cut the paper into equal pieces.

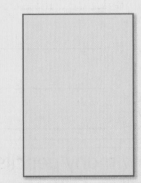

2 equal pieces   3 equal pieces   4 equal pieces   6 equal pieces

We Use Bottles and Jars

What are 3 things that you can do with an empty jar?

1. _____

2. _____

3. _____

Unscramble the letters to make the names of things that come in bottles.

ASOD _____

PECKUTH _____

VILEO LIO _____

PEMAL RUSPY _____

PALEP CEJUI _____

Each answer rhymes with **jar**.

in the sky _____

not near _____

drive it _____

mark on skin _____

put on roads _____

Unscramble the words to make a sentence.

| of | party | bottles | for | bought | seven | the | we | soda |

_____

Analyze

Unlock the Answers!

Each key opens a lock. Together, that key and lock will form a 4-letter word. Match the keys and locks, and then write the words on the lines. Use each key and each lock only **one** time.

RE AN HA LT SA IP

TA BE CO

WH TR VE SL RP

FL WA

EE ME AT EN

_____   _____   _____

_____   _____   _____

_____   _____

Skill Sharpeners: Critical Thinking • EMC 3253 • © Evan-Moor Corp.

What's Inside?

The words listed below name things that can be found in bottles or jars. Use the words to fill the puzzle.

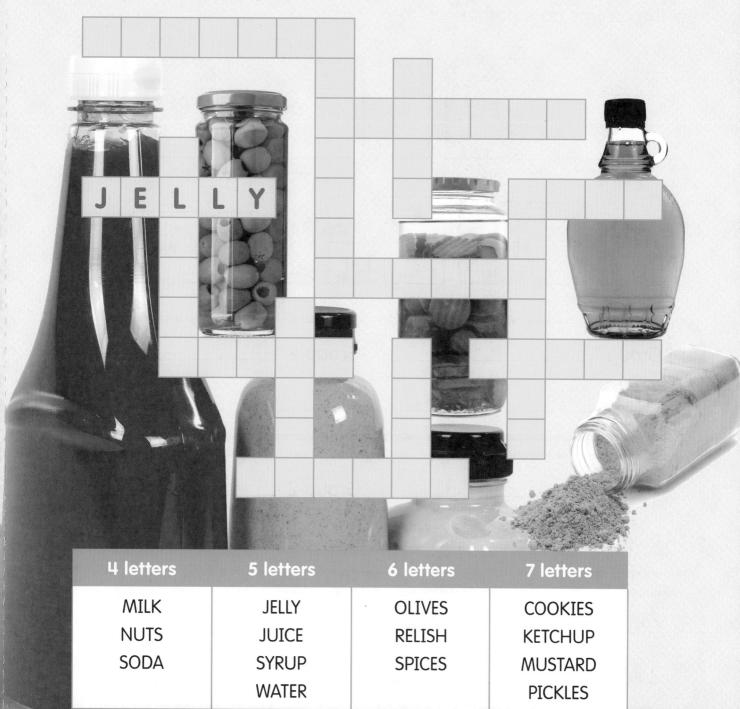

4 letters	5 letters	6 letters	7 letters
MILK	JELLY	OLIVES	COOKIES
NUTS	JUICE	RELISH	KETCHUP
SODA	SYRUP	SPICES	MUSTARD
	WATER		PICKLES

Originate

Boxes

Show 3 different ways to divide the boxes into groups. Each time, write the letters to show the 2 groups you made. Then write the rule that tells how the groups go together.

A B C D E F

G H I J K L M N

Group 1: _____ Group 2: _____

Rule: _____

Group 1: _____ Group 2: _____

Rule: _____

Group 1: _____ Group 2: _____

Rule: _____

Skill Sharpeners: Critical Thinking • EMC 3253 • © Evan-Moor Corp.

It's All Paper!

Answer each clue with the name of something that is made from paper. Then unscramble the letters in the boxes to complete the sentence at the bottom of the page.

drink from it ☐ ____ ____

hang this type of picture on the wall ____ ____ ____ ____ ____ ☐

on a bottle or jar ☐ ____ ____ ____

use to blow your nose ☐ ____ ____ ____ ____ ____

eat off it ____ ____ ____ ☐ ____

use to clean up a spill ____ ____ ____ ☐ ____

also called a bag ____ ____ ☐ ____

funny story told in pictures ____ ____ ____ ☐ ____

use to look up words ____ ____ ____ ____ ____ ____ ____ ☐

When you are done with paper, you should

____ ____ ____ ____ ____ ____ ____ ____ ____ ____ ____ ____ !

Create

My Box

Make a box to store your special things.

What You Need:

- markers or crayons
- scissors
- tape or glue

What You Do:

1. Carefully remove page 53 from book. Write your name under **My Box**.

2. Cut out the box along the dotted lines. Cut slits on the four dotted lines between the glue tab and the box sides (a). Fold where indicated along the solid lines (b). Glue or tape the tabs where indicated (c).

3. Place your favorite things in the box.

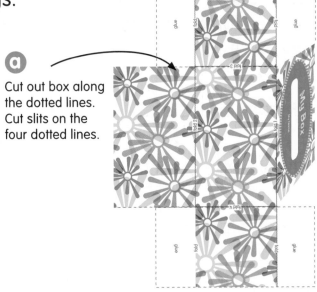

a Cut out box along the dotted lines. Cut slits on the four dotted lines.

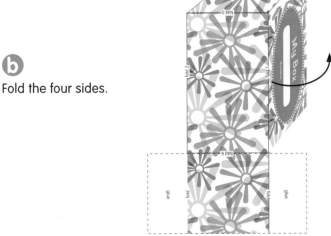

b Fold the four sides.

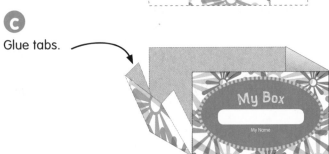

c Glue tabs.

Fill in the information. Cut on the lines. Fold where shown.
Tape or glue to make a box.

Things We Like

✓ I Did It! Check each activity as you complete it.

Be on the Lookout!

How many things that **you like** can you find on pages 57–62? Count them and write the number here: _____

Facts About Things We Like

Read about things we like, then answer the questions on the following pages.

Have you ever thought about how many different things you like? You may like pets, parties, presents, foods, and even superheroes! Our world is full of so many things to like!

Do you ever wonder why you like certain animals or why you like to do certain things? It may not be something you think about often, but you may learn something about yourself if you give it some thought.

For example, why do you like to play with cats more than dogs? Why do you like going to parties and playing games? Why do you like some sweets but not others?

Our personality helps form our likes and dislikes. Sometimes the things we like just come naturally to us. For example, who's your favorite superhero? You probably like that character for reasons that are all your own. You may not have even thought about why you like that superhero...you just do.

As you learn more and do more, you may find out that there are more and more things you like. That's a good thing!

Do your friends like the same things you do, or do they like different things? It's okay to like different things. What you like is part of what makes you **you**!

Tell What You Know

Things We Like

If you could meet a superhero, who would it be? Explain why.

_____

_____

If you had to choose between a party and a present, what would you choose? Explain why.

_____

_____

Write two things you like. Then number the list from 1 to 6. The one you like the most should be number 1.

_____ _____

_____ _____

_____ pets

_____ parties

_____ superheroes

_____ presents

Doug's dog, Kacey, had a litter of puppies three years ago. There were 4 black puppies, 2 white puppies, and 6 tan puppies. This year, Doug's dog had another litter of puppies, but this time it was only half the size. Doug's family kept all of the puppies both times. How many dogs does Doug's family have now?

_____

We Like Pets

Would you rather own a dog or a cat? _____

Why? _____

What kind of pet are they?

iguana, snake, turtle _____

canary, parrot, dove _____

rat, gerbil, hamster _____

beagle, Lab, hound _____

Raul has 2 kinds of pets: dogs and birds. One day, Raul counted his pets' heads and legs. There were 9 heads and 22 legs. How many dogs and birds does Raul have?

_____ dogs

_____ birds

Write 1 good thing and 1 bad thing about owning each kind of pet.

Pet	☺ Good Thing	☹ Bad Thing
Fish		
Hamster		
Parakeet		
Dog		

Skill Sharpeners: Critical Thinking • EMC 3253 • © Evan-Moor Corp.

Determine

We Like Parties

The answer is **a big party**. What is the question?

_____

Write a sentence using the words **party**, **cake**, and **sister**.

_____

These are things you might do at a party. Number them from 1 to 6. The one you like most should be number 1.

_____ see friends

_____ play games

_____ wear special clothes

_____ meet new people

_____ eat yummy food

_____ see presents opened

Nikki had a lot of balloons at her party.

- There were 3 times as many **red** balloons as **blue** balloons.

- There were 6 more **green** balloons than **blue** balloons.

- There were 14 **green** balloons.

How many balloons of each color were there?

_____ red balloons

_____ blue balloons

_____ green balloons

Things   59

Explain

We Like Presents

What is the best present that you ever got? _____

Why? _____

What is the best present that you ever gave? _____

Why? _____

You receive a present in a long, skinny box. What are 4 things that might be inside?

1. _____

2. _____

3. _____

4. _____

Janie made her mom a present. It took her 4½ hours to make it. She made the card, too. That took 45 minutes. It took 8 minutes to wrap the gift. Janie started her project at 10:15 in the morning. At what time did she finish?

_____

What do you think the expression "good things come in small packages" means?

_____

What are 3 good things that could come in small packages?

1. _____   2. _____   3. _____

Specify

We Like Superheroes

If you could have one superpower, what would it be? _____

Why? _____

ANALOGIES

Spiderman : red :: The Incredible Hulk : _____

Clark Kent : Superman :: Bruce Wayne : _____

Wonder Woman : invisible plane :: Batman : _____

How do you think our world might be different if superheroes really existed?

_____

_____

If superheroes did exist, would you want to be one? _____

Why or why not? _____

Supergirl has had a busy day. First, she flew 1,247 miles from her home in Metropolis to New York, where she saved a little girl from being run over by a taxi. Next, she sped 3,628 miles to Paris to keep an earthquake from tumbling the Eiffel Tower. After that, it was 8,493 miles to China, where she arrived just in time to catch a man who'd fallen off the Great Wall. Then she flew 4,586 miles to Australia to capture some escaped criminals. Finally, she flew 9,364 miles home to Metropolis. How many miles did she fly altogether? _____ miles

Compute

Word Problems

Mrs. Rock is planning an ice-cream party for her class. She needs one cone for each of her 25 students and one cone for herself. There are 10 ice-cream cones in a box.

1. How many boxes of cones should she buy?

   _____ boxes of cones

2. How many cones will be left over?

   _____ cones left over

Mrs. Rock wants to know how much ice cream she will need. She will give each of her 25 students and herself two scoops of ice cream. How many scoops of ice cream will she need?

_____ scoops

More people like chocolate ice cream than rocky road. The same number of people like rocky road and strawberry. More people like strawberry than vanilla.

1. The flavor that most like is:

   _____

2. The flavor that fewest like is:

   _____

Mrs. Rock went to the store to buy the ice cream. She received 3 coins that equal 36¢ in change. Which coins did she receive?

_____

_____

_____

Skill Sharpeners: Critical Thinking • EMC 3253 • © Evan-Moor Corp.

Whose Pet?

Each of these 6 children has a different pet. Read the clues.
Then write the child's name under his or her pet.
Hint: You will need to read the clues at least 2 times.

| Charlie | Claire | Jack | Kate | Sawyer | Shannon |

- Kate is allergic to dogs.

- Jack's pet does not have legs.

- Shannon's pet lives in a cage.

- Kate's pet has 4 legs.

- Charlie and Sawyer each have a kind of pet
  that begins with the same letter as their names.

Infer

Where's the Party?

James is going to a party, but there is something wrong with the directions. Help him find the party by rewriting the directions with the spaces in the correct places.

Dir ecti onst oth ep arty:

_____

Dri venor thdo wnMa inStreet.

_____

Tur nlef tonEl mAve nue.

_____

Dri vef iveb locks.

_____

Loo kfo rth ere dho us e.

_____

Yo ua reh ere! Co meo nin!

_____

ANALOGIES

Eat is to **cake** as _____ is to **soda**.

Hit is to **piñata** as _____ is to **donkey**.

Hokeypokey is to **dance** as _____ is to **game**.

P is for party.

How many **p**'s were on this page

before you started to write? _____

Skill Sharpeners: Critical Thinking • EMC 3253 • © Evan-Moor Corp.

How Many Superheroes?

How many superheroes can you name?

1. _____   5. _____

2. _____   6. _____

3. _____   7. _____

4. _____   8. _____

Number the superpowers from 1 to 8. The one you think is best should be number 1.

_____ superstrength

_____ invisibility

_____ flight

_____ shape-shifting

_____ time travel

_____ X-ray vision

_____ weather control

_____ underwater breathing

Batman captured 11 bad guys on Tuesday. On Wednesday and Thursday, he captured a total of 23 bad guys. He captured a total of 18 bad guys on Tuesday and Wednesday. How many bad guys did Batman capture on each day?

Tuesday: _____

Wednesday: _____

Thursday: _____

How many altogether? _____

Write a sentence about a superhero. Use exactly 10 words.

_____

Create

My Hero!

Write a comic book story about your own real-life hero!

What You Need:

- markers or crayons
- scissors
- tape or glue
- paper fasteners
- white paper
- stapler

What You Do:

1. Carefully remove pages 67 and 69 from the book.

2. Color the cape, body, arms, and legs of your superhero, then cut out along the outside lines. Use fasteners to attach arms and legs to body.

3. Cut out a hairpiece or face-mask decoration, and a chest emblem from page 69. Glue them to your superhero.

4. Cut out a minibook cover. Cut several blank pieces of paper the same size and staple them together. Write about your superhero!

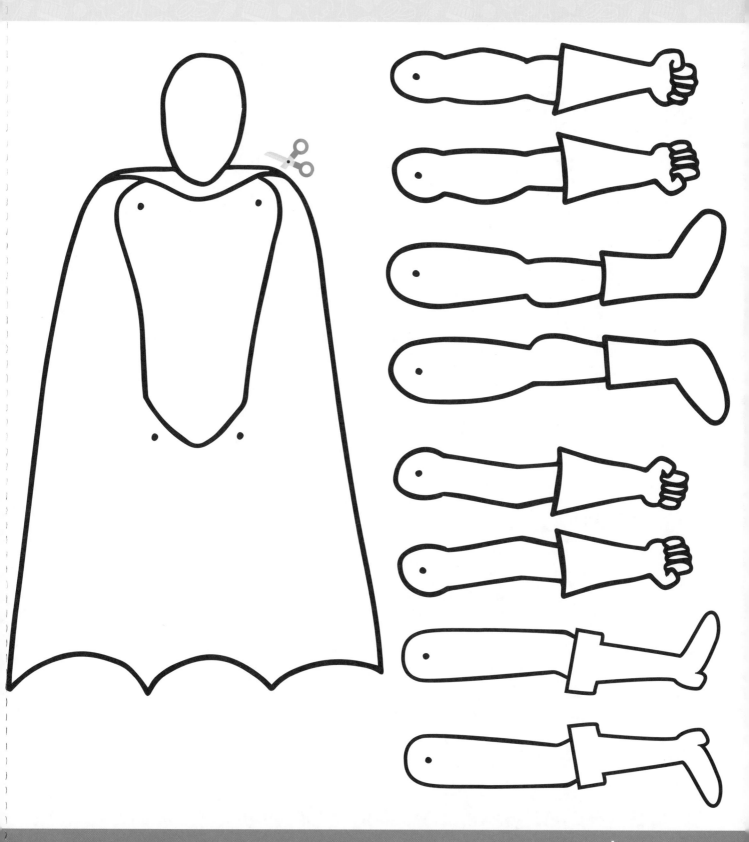

At Home

✓ I Did It! Check each activity as you complete it.

Be on the Lookout!

How many times can you find the word **family** on pages 73–78? Count and write the number here: _____

Facts About Home

Read these facts about home, then answer the questions on the following pages.

Have you ever heard the saying, "Home, sweet home"? This is just another way of saying that it's nice to be home! A lot of the people and things we love are at home.

What do you like about being at home?

What do you like best about being at home? Maybe you like to play with your brothers and sisters or spend time with your mom and dad. Maybe you have a pet you like to play with. Spending time with family is part of what makes being at home special.

Your bedroom is another thing that makes home special. Your toys, your books, and your favorite things are in your bedroom. Think about what you like best about your room. Is it how it looks? Is it your comfortable bed? Maybe you like to have a quiet place where you can think about your day or what you'd like to do when you grow up.

Mealtime can be a special time at home. Families gather around the table to eat the food mom or dad has prepared. It's a time to visit with each other and share stories about your day.

How do you help at home?

There's a lot to do to make home a special place. Chores like cleaning, cooking, and yardwork have to be done. Who does these chores at your house? How do you help? When families work together to do chores, it makes them easier and more fun for everyone. Maybe you can help set the dinner table or clear the places. Maybe you can pull weeds out of the flower garden. Maybe you can water the vegetable garden or the houseplants. Think about what you can do so that when you come home every day you say, "Home, sweet home!"

Family Tree

How many people are in your immediate family?

_____

How many people are in your family, including grandparents, aunts, uncles, and cousins?

_____

These **5** words describe my:

father

1. _____
2. _____
3. _____
4. _____
5. _____

mother

1. _____
2. _____
3. _____
4. _____
5. _____

You are a son or a daughter.
What other family roles do you have?

_____

_____

_____

_____

How are you the same as your father?

_____

_____

How are you different from your father?

_____

_____

How are you the same as your mother?

_____

_____

How are you different from your mother?

_____

_____

At the Dinner Table

Think about the table where you usually eat dinner.

What shape is it? _____ How many legs does it have? _____

What is it made out of? _____

When you sit at your usual spot at the table, what do you see…

straight ahead? _____

to the left? _____

to the right? _____

Where does each person sit? Label the chairs.

- Mom sits at the west end of the table, and Dad sits at the east end of the table.
- The twins, Lily and Susie, sit across from each other.
- Grandma sits to the left of Dad.
- Ben sits next to Susie.
- Lily sits to the right of Mom.

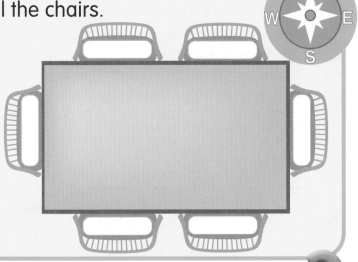

Dinnertime is a good time to catch up with your family. What are 3 questions you could ask to make dinnertime more interesting?

1. _____

2. _____

3. _____

Skill Sharpeners: Critical Thinking • EMC 3253 • © Evan-Moor Corp.

Rate

My Room

Some kids share a room with a brother or a sister.
Write 3 advantages and 3 disadvantages of sharing a room.

Advantages	Disadvantages

ANALOGIES

shelves : books :: closet : _____

desk : study :: bed : _____

posters : wall :: rug : _____

pillow : soft :: desk : _____

If these things could talk, what would they say?

Your floor: _____

Your closet: _____

Your pillow: _____

Rate your room. Fill in a number on the scale for each.

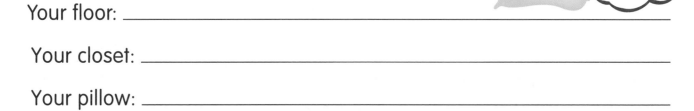

messy	1	2	3	4	5	neat
boring	1	2	3	4	5	interesting
uncomfortable	1	2	3	4	5	comfortable

Describe

I Help at Home

Mom
Dad
Grandma
Grandpa
Brother
Sister
Me

Who in your family needs the most help? _____

Why? _____

_____

SYNONYMS

Help is a synonym for **assist**. Write a synonym for each word below.

job _____

quick _____

ask _____

problem _____

shy _____

thankful _____

Last night, Terry helped his little sister with her homework. Use the clues to find out how long it took.

- It took less than an hour, but more than half an hour.
- The number of minutes is divisible by 5 by not by 10.
- The sum of the digits is 9.

Terry helped his sister for

_____ minutes.

Kate, Emily, and Lucy are working on a school project together. Kate is not doing her share of the work. In fact, she is not helping at all. What are 3 things that Emily and Lucy can do to solve this problem?

1. _____

2. _____

3. _____

Skill Sharpeners: Critical Thinking • EMC 3253 • © Evan-Moor Corp.

Determine

A Place for Me

Write 6 adjectives to describe your room.

1. _____ 2. _____ 3. _____

4. _____ 5. _____ 6. _____

Unscramble these things that you would probably find in a bedroom. Then write the words in the grid.

DEB _____

KEDS _____

OROD _____

SKOBO _____

WILOPL _____

LETCOS _____

DONWWI _____

SLESVEH _____

SERRDES _____

STEHLOC _____

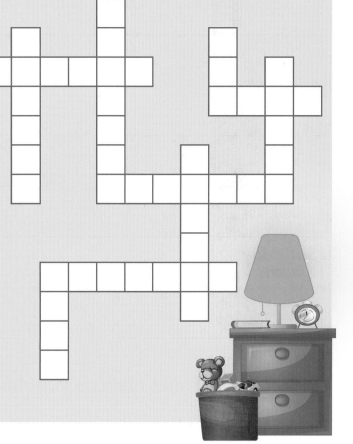

If you were moving and you could take only 3 things from your room, what would you take?

1. _____

2. _____

3. _____

Produce

Let's Eat!

It's Rainbow Week at the Smith house! During Rainbow Week, the family eats a different color meal each night. Each meal must contain a main dish, a side dish, a vegetable, and a beverage. Every item must be the correct color. Can you think of a menu for each night?

	Main Dish	Side Dish	Vegetable	Beverage
Monday yellow				
Tuesday red				
Wednesday green				
Thursday brown				
Friday orange				
Saturday white				
Sunday purple				

Which night's dinner menu is your favorite? _____

Would you want to have Rainbow Week at your house? ◯ YES ◯ NO

Why or why not? _____

_____

Secret Number

Read the clues below to find the secret number. Each clue will help you eliminate one or more numbers. Cross out each number that you eliminate.

- This number is odd
- This number has 2 digits
- The digits of this number, added together, have a sum that is greater than 11.

- The digit **9** does <u>not</u> appear in this number.
- The first digit of this number is one greater than the second digit.

1	2	3	4	5	6	7	8	9	10
11	12	13	14	15	16	17	18	19	20
21	22	23	24	25	26	27	28	29	30
31	32	33	34	35	36	37	38	39	40
41	42	43	44	45	46	47	48	49	50
51	52	53	54	55	56	57	58	59	60
61	62	63	64	65	66	67	68	69	70
71	72	73	74	75	76	77	78	79	80
81	82	83	84	85	86	87	88	89	90
91	92	93	94	95	96	97	98	99	100

The secret number is _____

Solve

Food for Thought

Dad made baked potatoes. If he puts 1 potato on everyone's plate, he will have one extra potato. If he puts 2 potatoes on everyone's plate, one person will not get any potatoes at all. How many people are in Dad's family, and how many baked potatoes did he make?

Julia's family eats rice with dinner every third night. They have peas every fourth night. It is Monday night, and Julia's family is eating both rice and peas. On what day of the week will they next eat rice and peas in the same meal?

_____

_____ people

_____ potatoes

What are ❸ other things you could use the dinner table for besides eating?

❶ _____

❷ _____

❸ _____

Create the most disgusting dinner that you can imagine.

Main dish: _____

Side dish: _____

Vegetable: _____

Beverage: _____

For $100, would you eat the dinner that you created?

◯ YES ◯ NO

What is the most disgusting thing that you have ever eaten?

_____

Categorize

My Family

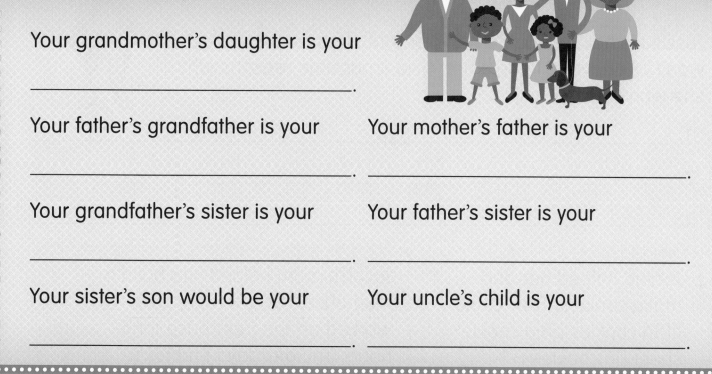

Your grandmother's daughter is your

_____.

Your father's grandfather is your

_____.

Your mother's father is your

_____.

Your grandfather's sister is your

_____.

Your father's sister is your

_____.

Your sister's son would be your

_____.

Your uncle's child is your

_____.

Being the oldest or the youngest or an only child has advantages and disadvantages. Fill in the chart to show at least one for each.

	Advantages	Disadvantages
Oldest		
Youngest		
Only child		

If you could choose, would you want to be the oldest, the youngest, or an only child?

_____ Why? _____

Analyze

What Do You Think?

Jessica is having trouble with her math homework, but she won't ask anyone to help her. Give 3 possible reasons why she won't ask for help.

1. _____

2. _____

3. _____

Joanie helped her dad make cookies. They could fit 16 cookies on a cookie sheet (16 cookies = 1 batch). They had enough dough to make 200 cookies. How many batches did they make?

_____ batches

Jacob's mom helped him build a treehouse. For 3 weeks, they worked on the treehouse for 6 hours on Saturdays and for 2 hours after school on Mondays, Wednesdays, and Fridays. How many hours did Jacob work on the treehouse? _____ hours

Name something that you once needed help with but do **not** need help with now.

_____

Name something that you need help with now but probably will **not** need help with when you are a little older.

_____

Skill Sharpeners: Critical Thinking • EMC 3253 • © Evan-Moor Corp.

Bedroom Words

Use the clues to solve the crossword puzzle.
The words are all things that can be found in a bedroom.

DOWN

1 Place for clothes
3 On the bed
4 Read this
7 On the wall
9 Has drawers
11 Put it together
13 Open it to leave
14 On the floor
15 Place for books
18 Where you sleep

ACROSS

2 Lights up the room
5 Play with this
6 Tells the time
8 See outside
10 Prize for winning
12 Dirty clothes go here
13 Do homework here
15 For your feet
16 Play it with a friend
17 Nice to hug

Create

My Family Tree

Create a family tree that tells the names of the people in your family.

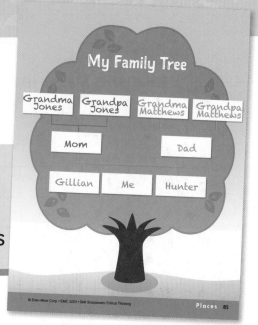

What You Need:

- scissors
- a pencil or pen
- colored pencils or pens
- the boxes below
- a list of family members' names

What You Do:

1. Write the names of your family members in the boxes below. Write one person's name in each box. Include the names of your brothers and sisters, your parents (including the last name that your mom grew up with), and your grandparents. Cut out the boxes.

2. Carefully remove page 85 from the book. Glue the names of your family members to the family tree on that page. You and your siblings will be on the bottom row. Your parents are in the row above you, and your grandparents are in the row above them. Look at the example for help.

Skill Sharpeners: Critical Thinking • EMC 3253 • © Evan-Moor Corp.

My Family Tree

At School

✓ I Did It! Check each activity as you complete it.

Be on the Lookout!

How many times can you find the word **school** on pages 89–96? Count and write the number here: _____

Facts About School

Read these facts about school, then answer the questions on the following pages.

You spend a lot of your time at school. School is a place to learn, to discover, to make friends, and to have fun. The people who work at the school are there to help you do these things.

What do you like about being at school?

What do you like best about being at school? Maybe you like to learn about science or history. Maybe math is your favorite subject. What do you like to learn about? Making projects at school is fun. Some projects use arts and crafts materials. Other projects use building materials or plant materials. What projects have you done at school? What projects would you like to do?

Recess is a fun time at school. You can enjoy being outside, you can play sports, and you can visit with your friends while you eat your snack. Recess is a time for you to take a break from learning and get out some of your energy. What do you like to do at recess?

Many schools plan field trips to visit places in the community. There may be field trips to a museum, to a factory, to a farm, or to an amusement park. Some field trips help you learn about life in the past. Some field trips teach you about jobs in your community. Other field trips are just to have fun! Have you ever been on a field trip? Where did you go?

When do you do your homework?

Most schools give students work to complete at home. There's a lot to learn, and sometimes you can't fit all of it into the school day. That's where homework comes in. Finding a quiet place at home to do your homework is important. Thinking about when you will do your homework is also important. When will your mind be ready to focus? After you play outside? After you have a snack? Or are you ready to do your homework as soon as you get home? Doing your homework is an important part of being a good student. It feels good to go to school with your homework complete and ready to start a new day!

Spectacular School Days!

What is the best thing about starting school each year?

_____

What is the hardest thing about starting school each year?

_____

Krystal catches the bus at 8:30. It takes her 10 minutes to walk to the bus stop, 5 minutes to get her school stuff together, 15 minutes to eat breakfast, and 25 minutes to bathe and get dressed. At what time does Krystal need to get up?

_____

At what time do you get up for school?

_____

Do you get up earlier or later than Krystal?

_____

How much earlier or later do you get up?

_____

Write 2 **school** things that start with each letter.

C _____ and _____

T _____ and _____

In Your Classroom

Picture your classroom. Name something in your classroom that is:

round _____

sharp _____

soft _____

colorful _____

tiny _____

The purpose of a classroom is to provide a place for learning. What are the 5 most important things in your classroom that help you learn?

1. _____

2. _____

3. _____

4. _____

5. _____

If your desk could talk, what would it say? Write it down.

Add as many words as you can.

pencil, crayon, chalk, _____

teacher, janitor, nurse, _____

math, spelling, science, _____

Skill Sharpeners: Critical Thinking • EMC 3253 • © Evan-Moor Corp.

The First Day

Oh dear, it is only the first day of school, and Alex has already forgotten something important! For each clue, find the letter that is in the first boldfaced word but <u>not</u> in the second boldfaced word. Then write the letters in order on the lines at the bottom of this page to find out what Alex forgot.

- It is in **CATCH** but not in **CACTUS**.

- It is in **KITE** but not in **TAKE**.

- It is in **CHEST** but not in **CHEAT**.

- It is in **SLIP** but not in **PIES**.

- It is in **PLUS** but not in **SLAP**.

- It is in **NICE** but not in **CITIES**.

- It is in **RICE** but not in **TIRES**.

- It is in **HARP** but not in **PARTY**.

What can Alex do to solve his problem?

_____

_____

_____

_____

_____

Alex forgot

_____ _____ _____

_____ _____ _____ _____ _____.

Give Your Opinion

Books

Do you like to read? 👍 _____ 👎 _____

Why or why not? _____

Think about the books that you have read, or that someone has read to you. Which one was the…

funniest? _____

scariest? _____

longest? _____

Taylor got 12 books from the library. One-third of them were about birds. One-fourth of them were about cats. The rest were about monkeys. How many of the books were about monkeys?

_____ monkey books

Which kinds of books have you read? Write **R** for the ones you have read. Write **N** for the ones you have <u>not</u> read.

_____ chapter books

_____ picture books

_____ comic books

_____ animal books

_____ biographies

_____ science books

_____ manga

_____ joke books

_____ fantasy books

_____ nonfiction books

Infer

Homework

The answer is **my homework**. What is the question?

_____

Why do teachers give homework? List 2 reasons.

1. _____

2. _____

What kind of homework did Juan get? Cross out the letters of the kinds of homework he did <u>not</u> get to find the kind he <u>did</u> get.

G E Z S M I S L N A P E I U T E C N H L I C Q

He did not get **SPELLING**.

He did not get **SCIENCE**.

He did not have to study for a **QUIZ**.

Juan's homework was

_____.

Marta eats a snack before she does her homework.
She feeds her cat after she goes to soccer practice.
She does her homework before soccer practice.
Write the order of Marta's activities.

First: _____

Second: _____

Third: _____

Fourth: _____

Compute

Word Problems

Sue is taller than Allison but shorter than Dana. Virginia is the same height as Allison. Mary is taller than Dana. Who is the tallest? Draw pictures to help you find the answer.

_____ is tallest.

Guess the mystery number. The number is greater than 10 and less than 18. The number is the sum of two identical odd numbers. What is the number? Show how you found your answer.

_____

Guess the mystery number. The number is a multiple of 5. The number is a two-digit number ending in a 5. The number is less than 25.

_____

Figure out whether James is hiding in the living room, the garage, the bedroom, the kitchen, or the basement. Clues: He didn't just cook up a good place to hide. He never takes hiding lying down. He won't need to buckle up where he's hiding. You won't have to dig deep to find him.

James is hiding in the

_____.

Skill Sharpeners: Critical Thinking • EMC 3253 • © Evan-Moor Corp.

Describe

On a Field Trip

If you could plan a field trip for your class, where would you go?

_____

Why? _____

Pilar's class went on a field trip to the aquarium. It took 42 minutes to get there on the bus. It took 9 minutes to get everyone organized once they got there. They looked at fish for 67 minutes, and then they had lunch for 38 minutes. After lunch, they watched the seals eat for 13 minutes, and then they went to a special presentation about tide pools for 45 minutes. It took 8 minutes to load the bus, and the ride back to school took 48 minutes. The class left the school at 9:00 a.m. At what time did they return? _____

On the bus ride to the aquarium, James, Tim, Derek, Tonya, Jessica, and Dina sat in certain seats. Read the clues, and then write the children's names on their seats.

- Children with names that begin with the same letter sat together.
- The boys sat on the left.
- The children sat in alphabetical order, front to back.

Back

Front

SCHOOL BUS

Explain

Rules

What are 3 rules for your school?

1. _____

2. _____

3. _____

What are 3 different rules for your house?

1. _____

2. _____

3. _____

Use the clues to find the words.
Each word rhymes with this word:

RULE

use to fix things _____

swim here _____

chilly _____

holds thread _____

sit on this _____

unkind _____

silly person _____

place to learn _____

When Myron plays board games, he follows the rules only one-third of the time. He has played Monopoly 51 times. How many times has Myron not played by the rules?

_____ times

Do you always play by the rules? _____

Why or why not?

_____

_____

_____

Their Favorite Colors

There are four boys in your class. Use the clues below to find each boy's favorite color. When you know that a name and a color do not go with each other, make an **X** under the color and across from the name. When you know that a name and color do go together, write **YES** in that box.

	Blue	Green	Yellow	Red
Greg				
Ian				
Andy				
Fred				

Clues:

- Each boy has a different color as his favorite.

- Greg and Ian don't like blue.

- Ian and Andy don't like green.

- Greg and Andy don't like yellow.

- Andy, Greg, and Fred don't like red.

Rank

Where Should We Go?

The names of some places a class might go on a field trip are listed below. Number them from 1 to 6 according to how much you would like going on each trip.

_____ a science museum

_____ to see a play

_____ an art museum

_____ the aquarium

_____ the zoo

_____ a tour of a candy factory

Find the answer to each clue by using the letters in these words:

FIELD TRIP

inside a peach	_____
sleepy	_____
to lose weight	_____
group of lions	_____
fib	_____
scarlet	_____
dessert	_____
heap	_____
turn over	_____
ran away	_____
for fingernails	_____

Everyone has to turn in a permission slip to go on the field trip. On Monday, half the class turned in their slips. On Tuesday, 9 more students turned in their slips. There are 28 students in the class. How many students have not yet turned in their slips?

_____ students

What are 2 things you should <u>never</u> do on a field trip?

1. _____

2. _____

Skill Sharpeners: Critical Thinking • EMC 3253 • © Evan-Moor Corp.

Help!

Ryan has gotten separated from his class on the field trip.
He needs to make it back to the bus before it leaves.

To help Ryan get back to the bus, start at the square in the upper-left corner. Move the same number of squares as the number shown (2). Move in a straight line in any direction. After you move two squares, move the same number of squares as the number shown in the box you are on.

Can you make a path that will take Ryan to the bus? Color the path.

2	7	3	6	1	5	9	2	1	8	4	3
5	2	2	6	3	1	3	7	5	2	9	1
7	8	1	6	2	7	1	5	2	6	6	2
1	3	4	2	7	2	4	4	7	1	1	7
2	7	3	6	1	3	9	2	1	8	4	3
1	3	4	2	7	2	4	4	7	2	1	7
5	2	2	6	3	1	3	7	5	2	9	1
7	8	1	6	2	4	3	2	2	4	6	2
2	7	3	6	1	4	9	2	1	2	4	6
1	3	4	2	7	2	3	8	3	2	1	2
7	8	1	6	2	1	1	4	2	6	6	1
5	2	2	8	3	1	3	5	3	2	3	1

Create

Origami School

Create a folded paper schoolhouse while you learn origami!

What You Need:

- paper square on page 101
- scissors

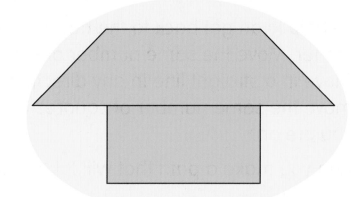

What You Do:

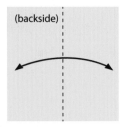

1 Cut out the square on page 101. Fold the paper in half. Open.

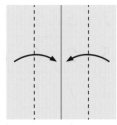

2 Fold the two sides into the center fold line.

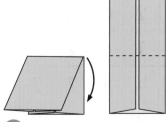

3 Fold top to bottom in half. Open.

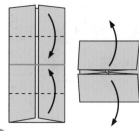

4 Fold top and bottom in to meet centerfold line. Open.

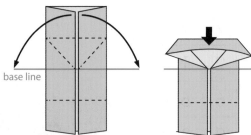

5 Take looser corner and fold down to base line. (see red line.) Do the same on the other side.

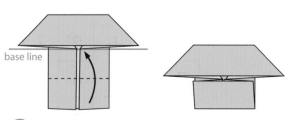

7 Fold bottom in to meet base line.

Origami is the Japanese word for paper folding. ORI means to fold and KAMI means paper. Together, they have become the word **origami**.

Origami is an art form from Japan that has been handed down from parent to child through many generations.

Mother Nature

✓ I Did It! Check each activity as you complete it.

Be on the Lookout!

How many times can you find the word **Earth** on pages 104–117?
Count and write the number here: _____

Facts About Mother Nature

Read about Mother Nature, then answer the questions on the following pages.

Have you ever heard the expression "Mother Nature"? Do you wonder what this means? Saying **Mother Nature** is a way of saying that Earth takes care of us and gives us what we need to live, like a mother does. From its rainbows, to its night sky, to its sparkling bodies of water, Earth is an amazing planet that must be protected, just as we protect the people and things that we love.

How can you help protect Earth? There are many things you can do.

Reuse and Recycle

You probably have seen this symbol on bins at school and at home. Instead of putting paper, metal, plastic, glass, and other materials in the garbage can, you put it in the recycle bin. Why is the recycle bin better than the garbage can? Recycling is good for the environment, and saves energy, natural resources, and space in landfills. Garbage goes to landfills, and landfills pollute the air and the water.

Conserve Water

Many areas of the world don't get as much rain as they need. This causes people to have a drought, or water shortage. But people need to use water to keep their bodies clean. So how can we save, or conserve, water? When we take showers, we can turn off the faucet while we soap up our bodies. Similarly, when you wash your hands and brush your teeth, don't let the water run. Turn off the faucet while you wash or brush. Turn it on to rinse your hands or mouth.

Mother Nature's Helper

You can be Mother Nature's helper by protecting Earth. She will thank us with a beautiful, healthy planet.

Skill Sharpeners: Critical Thinking • EMC 3253 • © Evan-Moor Corp.

Mother Nature

How does recycling help the Earth?

_____

How does driving less help the Earth?

_____

How does using less electricity help the Earth?

_____

If you could fly around the Earth in an airplane, you would have to fly 24,900 miles. An airplane flies about 500 miles an hour. About how many hours would it take you to circle the Earth?

_____ hours

Where in the world are you?

Continent: _____

Country: _____

State: _____

County: _____

City: _____

Street: _____

Add 2 more each time, and then tell what they are.

Atlantic, Indian, _____, _____ What? _____

Australia, Asia, _____, _____ What? _____

France, Spain, Belgium, _____, _____ What? _____

Reuse and Recycle

When we reuse things instead of throwing them away, we save resources and we don't fill up landfills. How could you reuse each of these items?

soda bottle _____

egg carton _____

old magazines _____

torn shirt _____

SYNONYMS

Garbage is a synonym for **trash**. Write a synonym for each below.

bin _____

smelly _____

slimy _____

broken _____

soiled _____

disgusting _____

Mr. Smith takes out his garbage on Mondays and Thursdays. Mr. Jones takes out his garbage once every 3 days. Both men have taken out their garbage today. Today is Thursday, March 6. On what date will both men take out their garbage on the same day again?

_____

Fill in the can that shows what percentage of waste you think your family recycles weekly.

50%   33%   25%   20%

Water

What are **10** different things that we use water for?

1. _____
2. _____
3. _____
4. _____
5. _____

6. _____
7. _____
8. _____
9. _____
10. _____

Circle rain drops that add up to 16. You may circle as many raindrops as you like. Your circles can overlap. One example is done for you.

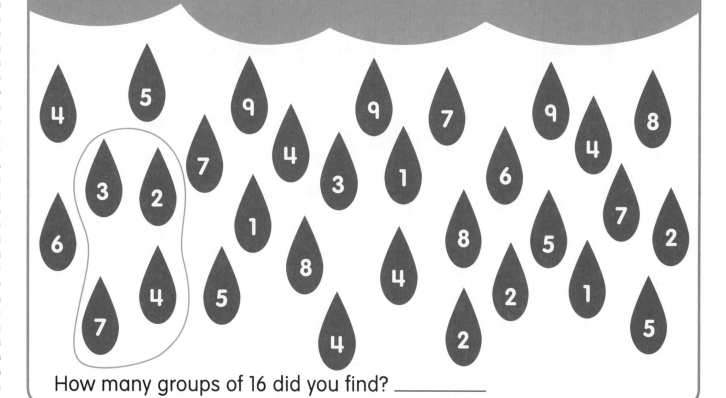

How many groups of 16 did you find? _____

Determine

Rainbows

The answer is **purple**. What is the question?

_____

The answer is **yellow and black**. What is the question?

_____

Unscramble the names of the colors, and then write them in the grid.

WORBN _____

GENER _____

TEWIH _____

PRECOP _____

GRONAE _____

LEPRUP _____   DRE _____   RAGY _____

LIVERS _____   LUBE _____   KINP _____

WOLELY _____   LOGD _____   CLKAB _____

The Night Sky

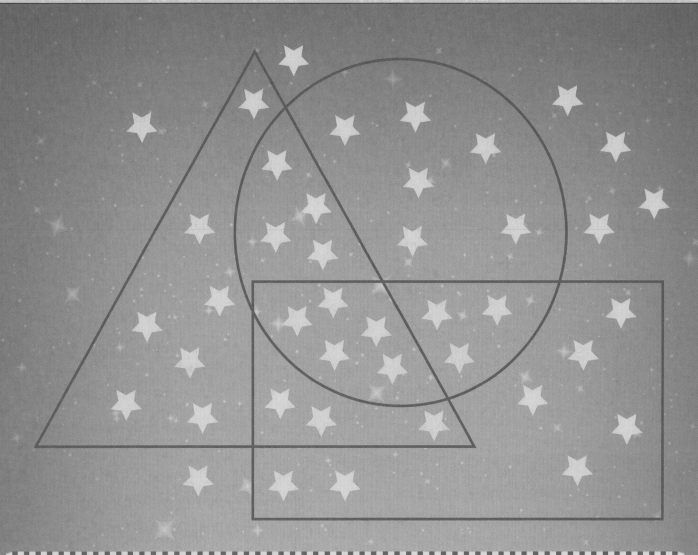

How many stars are in the shapes?

triangle only _____   triangle and circle _____

rectangle only _____   triangle and rectangle _____

circle only _____   all three shapes total _____

circle and rectangle _____   no shapes _____

Compute

Word Problems

Oceans can be deeper than the height of the tallest mountains. In the Pacific Ocean, the Mariana Trench is 35,840 feet deep. The tallest mountain, Mount Everest, is 29,035 feet tall. How much deeper is the Mariana Trench than Mount Everest is tall?

_____

feet deeper

The average depth of the Indian Ocean is 12,598 feet. The average depth of the Atlantic Ocean is 11,730 feet. How much deeper is the Indian Ocean than the Atlantic Ocean?

_____

feet deeper

The area of the continent of Antarctica is 5,400,000 square miles. The area of the Arctic Ocean is about 5,105,700 square miles. How much larger is the area of Antarctica than the area of the Arctic Ocean?

_____

square miles larger

The Pacific Ocean is about 64,186,300 square miles in area. The Atlantic Ocean is about 33,420,000 square miles in area. How many square miles are both oceans together?

_____

square miles

Skill Sharpeners: Critical Thinking • EMC 3253 • © Evan-Moor Corp.

Where on Earth?

Where is your favorite place on Earth? _____

If the Earth could talk, what do you think it would say?

Number the places from 1 to 8 according to how much you would like to visit them. The one you would like to visit the most should be number 1.

_____ China

_____ Africa

_____ Australia

_____ France

_____ Peru

_____ Egypt

_____ India

_____ Hawaii

A **natural resource** is something we use that comes from nature. Coal is an example of a natural resource. How many others can you name?

1. _____   4. _____   7. _____

2. _____   5. _____   8. _____

3. _____   6. _____   9. _____

Conclude

Garbage

Write a sentence that is **always** true about garbage.

_____

Write a sentence that is sometimes true about garbage.

_____

Write a sentence that is **never** true about garbage.

_____

Find the word for each clue. Each word is made from the letters in this word:

GARBAGE

use to carry things _____

to snatch _____

large, furry animal _____

how old you are _____

to boast _____

flat boat _____

Each person in the United States produces about 1,609 pounds of garbage a year! About how many pounds of garbage did your family produce last year?

_____ pounds

About how many pounds of garbage have you produced in your life so far?

_____ pounds

What are **2** ways that your family could produce less garbage?

1. _____

2. _____

Skill Sharpeners: Critical Thinking • EMC 3253 • © Evan-Moor Corp.

All Wet

The word **rain** contains the letters **r** and **n**. How many other words can you make that contain both of these letters? The **r** <u>must</u> come before the **n**. *Examples*: run, grant

1. _____   6. _____   11. _____

2. _____   7. _____   12. _____

3. _____   8. _____   13. _____

4. _____   9. _____   14. _____

5. _____   10. _____   15. _____

The word **wet** contains the letters **w** and **t**. See how many other words you can make that contain **w** and **t**. The **w** <u>must</u> come before the **t**.

1. _____   6. _____   11. _____

2. _____   7. _____   12. _____

3. _____   8. _____   13. _____

4. _____   9. _____   14. _____

5. _____   10. _____   15. _____

Categorize

Ocean Depths

The chart below shows the area and average depth of four of Earth's oceans.

Ocean	Area (in square miles)	Average Depth (in feet)
Arctic	5,105,700	3,407
Atlantic	33,420,000	11,730
Indian	28,350,500	12,598
Pacific	64,186,300	12,925

Use the chart to complete the following questions.

• Write the oceans in order from the largest area to the smallest area.

_____ _____ _____ _____

• What is the difference between the largest area and the smallest area?

_____

• Put the oceans in order from the greatest depth to the smallest depth.

_____ _____ _____ _____

• What is the difference between the greatest depth and the smallest depth?

_____

Skill Sharpeners: Critical Thinking • EMC 3253 • © Evan-Moor Corp.

What's in the Can?

Some archaeologists study the garbage of ancient cultures to learn about how people lived. What can you learn about the Smith family by studying their garbage? Write about it below.

Found in the Smith Family's Garbage and Recycling

- rice cakes bag
- diet soda bottle
- wilted lettuce leaves
- carrot peelings
- tomato stems
- broken mousetrap
- chocolate cake mix box
- frosting container
- 10 half-burned candles
- crumpled wrapping paper
- ice-cream carton
- school lunch calendar
- town pool schedule
- sugarless gum wrappers
- dead flowers
- *American Girl* magazine
- *Boys' Life* magazine
- 3 dog food cans
- large pizza box
- lice shampoo bottle
- tofu container
- nonfat yogurt container
- allergy pill bottle
- microwave popcorn bag
- broken Beatles CD
- veggie burger box
- hamburger bun bag
- onion skins
- 2 lottery tickets
- unidentifiable moldy stuff

What are 3 things that you know about this family?

1. _____

2. _____

3. _____

What are 3 things that are probably true about this family?

1. _____

2. _____

3. _____

What are 3 things that might be true about this family?

1. _____

2. _____

3. _____

Apply

Rainbow Colors

Here is a fun trick to play on your brain. Use **red**, **blue**, yellow, **green**, orange, **purple**, and **brown** to neatly color each of these color names. But do <u>not</u> color them with the correct colors. For example, do <u>not</u> color the word **red** with red. When you are done, try to say the colors of the words as fast as you can. Do not read the words, just say the colors. Can you do it?

RED YELLOW
PURPLE GREEN
ORANGE BLUE
BROWN PURPLE
GREEN ORANGE

Why do you think it is so hard to say the color names? _____

_____

Earth Day

Find the words hidden in the puzzle.

```
C L E A N A N I M A L S R
A C A R E E X T I N C T W
R I N E W N A Q L M P T O
E X R U A E M R I C E E R
C O N S E R V A T I O N L
Y X F E E G S P T H P O D
C Y Z U R Y O M E L L Z W
L G S S E R I M R X E O A
E E A P O L L U T I O N T
E N V I R O N M E N T E E
S E E V O L U N T E E R R
E C U D E R N O W P L E H
```

air	Earth	litter	recycle	volunteer
animals	energy	oxygen	reduce	water
care	environment	ozone	reuse	world
clean	extinct	people	save	
conservation	fuel	pollution	soil	

Create

Collage Container

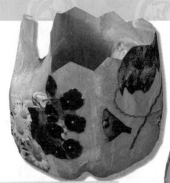

Reuse and recycle! Create a pot or bowl from a discarded container while learning about collage.

What You Need:

- colored tissue paper, wrapping paper, or magazine scraps
- glue
- old paintbrush
- used container such as a can, a plastic jug, or an oatmeal box

What You Do:

1. Make sure your container is clean and dry. If using a plastic jug, cut off the top to make it the desired size.

2. Cut up the tissue or wrapping paper into small pieces. Brush glue on the surface of the jug. Lay the paper pieces on the glued surface and brush glue over them. Let this layer dry completely.

3. Cut pictures from discarded magazines or junk mail. Add the pictures to the container, using the glue and the brush, as you did with the tissue or paper. Make sure all edges are glued securely. The key to good collage is overlapping the paper edges carefully.

4. When the collage is complete, set it aside to dry overnight. Then, you may want to spray on varnish to protect it. Ask an adult to help you do this.

Earth Needs Plants

✔ I Did It! Check each activity as you complete it.

Be on the Lookout!

Choose a word from this unit that **you think is important**.
Count the number of times you see it. Write the
number here: _____

Facts About Plants

Read about plants, then answer the questions on the following pages.

People rely on plants. We use plants for food, shelter, clothing, medicines, and even in the air we breathe.

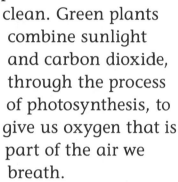

Plants keep our air and water clean. Green plants combine sunlight and carbon dioxide, through the process of photosynthesis, to give us oxygen that is part of the air we breath.

Plants are also part of the water cycle. Ninety percent or more of the water that is absorbed by a plant's roots goes back into the atmosphere.

Plants give us a lot of the food on Earth. Fruits, vegetables, and grains come from plants. Without plants, we would not have bread, rice, pasta, carrots, celery, apples, oranges, and bananas! Many people are growing plants to eat in their own gardens at home. Having your own garden helps Earth as well.

When you grow your own fruits and vegetables, you help cut down on pollution because big trucks do not need to deliver your food to stores. You also help reduce the amount of garbage that is created because you don't need to use packaging for your food. You can just pick it out of the ground or off of a plant and put it into a basket!

Trees are an important plant resource. Trees provide wood and materials to build homes and furniture. Trees are used to make countless items around your home and at your school. And, trees provide fruits that supply nutrients to our bodies. Without trees, Earth would be a very different place!

Plants

Write three reasons that Earth needs plants.

1. _____

2. _____

3. _____

What kinds of plants are most important to you? Explain why.

_____

_____

_____

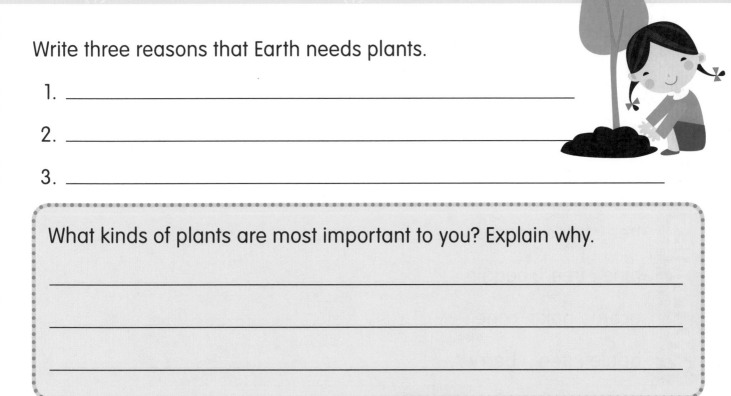

Olisa has a garden shop. She has 54 snapdragon plants. One customer wants to buy 42 snapdragon plants. There are 6 snapdragons in a pack.

How many packs should Olisa sell to her customer?

_____ packs

How many packs will Olisa have left?

_____ packs

Draw to finish the pattern.

Determine

Trees

Write 3 things that all trees have in common.

1 _____

2 _____

3 _____

ANALOGIES

tree : bark :: person : _____

pine : tree :: beagle : _____

acorn : oak :: cone : _____

apple : tree :: berry : _____

Would you like to live in a treehouse?

Why or why not?

_____

_____

_____

_____

_____

_____

Emily and Penelope were picking apples. Emily picked 3 times more apples than Penelope. Altogether they picked 168 apples. How many apples did each girl pick?

Emily: _____

Penelope: _____

In the Garden

You can plant **4** things in your garden.
What will you plant?

1. _____

2. _____

3. _____

4. _____

Jason planted 12 tomato plants.
There were about 15 tomatoes on
each of Jason's plants. About how
many tomatoes did Jason
harvest?

about _____ tomatoes

What are 3 things that Jason can
make with his tomatoes?

1. _____

2. _____

3. _____

Can you think of a vegetable for
each of these letters?

S _____

A _____

P _____

C _____

L _____

B _____

R _____

Z _____

Analyze

Eat Your Veggies

 Write a sentence that is true about vegetables.

_____

Write a sentence that is not true about vegetables.

_____

Write the letter or letters shared by the shapes.

carrot and eggplant _____

corn and tomato _____

eggplant, corn, and carrot _____

all 4 vegetables _____

1 vegetable each _____

Use the clues about vegetables to fill in the missing letters.

grows underground

C ____ ____ ____ ____ T

grows in heads

L ____ ____ ____ ____ ____ E

long and skinny

B ____ ____ ____

used to make pickles

C ____ ____ ____ ____ ____ R

Arbor Day

Read about Arbor Day and then complete the word search.

Arbor Day was started in 1872. It is a day to honor and plant trees. On April 10, 1872, Arbor Day was first celebrated in Nebraska with the planting of over one million trees. Arbor Day is celebrated in the United States on different days, but it is usually near April 22.

Trees provide us with many useful products. See how many you can find in the word search.

```
O X Y G E N I C E M Q T
P C B F L R U B B E R U
L O O U R S T U N D E R
Y C G R U U S A C I M P
W O L N K N I N I C A E
O N A I R O N T N I P N
O U S T D O O W N N L T
D T L U M B E R A E E I
C H A R C O A L M L S N
P A P E R N O T O M Y E
R O O T R E S I N S R B
C H E W I N G G U M U U
B X T C I D E R A M P G
C A R D B O A R D X P S
```

cardboard	cinnamon	furniture	nuts	resin
charcoal	coconut	lumber	oxygen	rubber
chewing gum	cork	maple syrup	paper	turpentine
cider	fruit	medicine	plywood	wood

Solve

Plant a Garden

Help Zoe plan her garden. Use the clues to find where each type of seed should be planted. Then write the vegetable names where they belong in the garden.

- Peas and beans should be planted in long rows.

- Zucchini should be planted west of the pumpkins.

- Tomatoes should be planted farthest to the east to get the morning sun.

- Peas are planted early, so they should be planted along the edge of the garden.

- Carrots should be planted south of the beans.

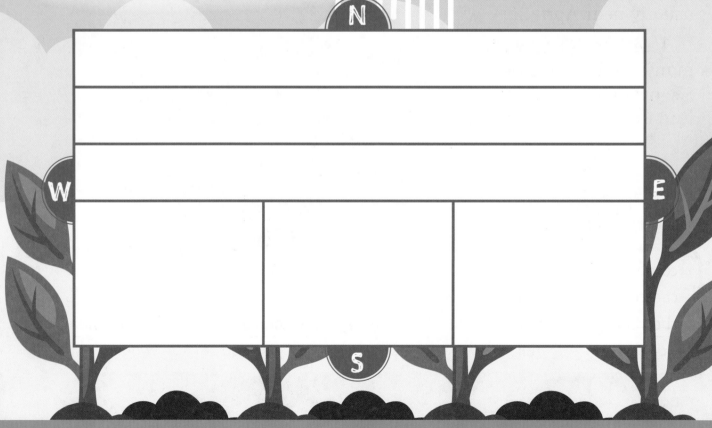

   Skill Sharpeners: Critical Thinking • EMC 3253 • © Evan-Moor Corp.

Do You Get It?

Can you decode this joke about trees?

A	B	C	D	E	F	G	H	I	J	K	L	M
Z	Y	X	W	V	U	T	S	R	Q	P	O	N
N	O	P	Q	R	S	T	U	V	W	X	Y	Z
M	L	K	J	I	H	G	F	E	D	C	B	A

D S Z G   W R W   G S V

____ ____ ____

G I V V   D V Z I   G L

____ ____ ____

G S V   H D R N N R M T

____ ____

K Z I G B

____ ?

Answer:

H D R N   G I F M P H

____ ____

Solve

About Trees

Use the clues to complete the crossword puzzle.

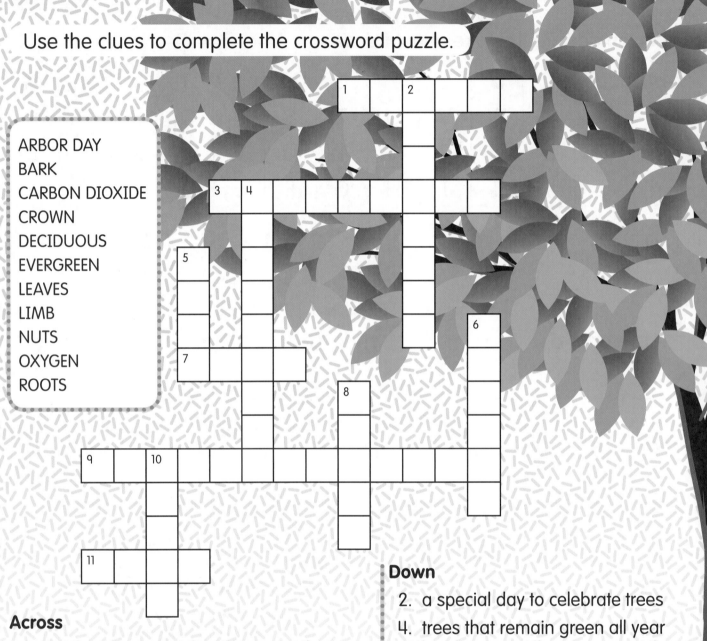

ARBOR DAY
BARK
CARBON DIOXIDE
CROWN
DECIDUOUS
EVERGREEN
LEAVES
LIMB
NUTS
OXYGEN
ROOTS

Across

1. the food-making part of a tree
3. trees that drop their leaves in the winter
7. the outer covering of a tree's trunk
9. trees absorb this, which helps clean the air
11. tree seeds that people eat

Down

2. a special day to celebrate trees
4. trees that remain green all year
5. another name for a tree branch
6. tree leaves release this into the air
8. the branches and leaves of a tree form a _____
10. these absorb water from the soil

Garden Games

Grant planted his favorite kind of vegetable. Cross out the letters of the vegetables that he did <u>not</u> plant to find the ones that he <u>did</u> plant.

E N Y S N Q R O L U E O A C I R O S C N H

He did not plant CELERY.

He did not plant ONIONS.

He did not plant CORN.

Grant planted _____.

Oh no! Bunnies are eating your vegetables. What can you do?

_____

_____

What vegetables are these?

 + **N** _____

 +  _____

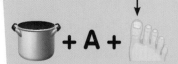 + **A** +  _____

In his garden, Alvin picked 27 zucchinis, 14 carrots, 22 apples, 18 onions, and 43 potatoes. How many vegetables did Alvin harvest?

_____ vegetables

Create

The Earth Needs Plants
Wall Art

Make a colorful wall-art flower for your room, as a reminder of how important plants are to us!

What You Need:

- scissors
- glue
- green colored paper
- colored pencils, crayons, or markers
- recycled cereal box

What You Do:

1. Carefully remove page 131. Color the earth art and glue it to a piece of cardboard from a cereal box to make it more stable. Cut it out.

2. Cut out the colored petals and glue them to the earth, from the back, to make a flower.

3. On each petal, write a reason why the earth needs plants.

4. Glue a stem to the earth from green paper. Cut out the green leaves and glue them to the stem.

THE EARTH NEEDS PLANTS

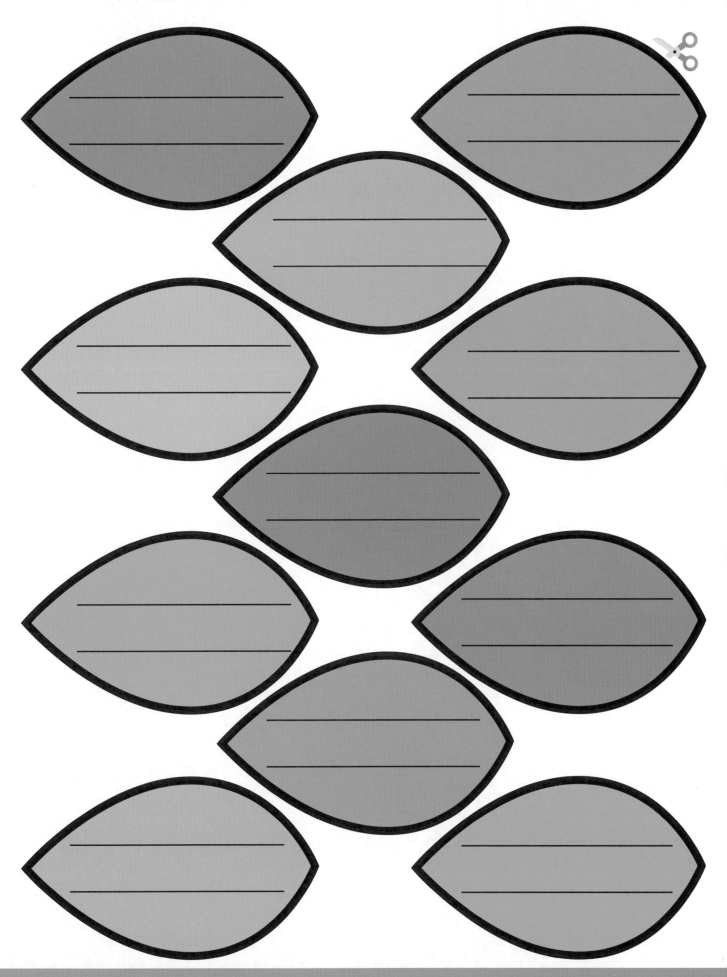

Answer Key

Page 9

Monkeys

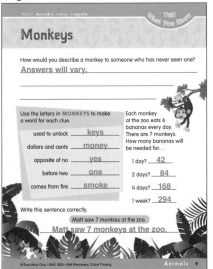

How would you describe a monkey to someone who has never seen one?

Answers will vary.

Use the letters in **MONKEYS** to make a word for each clue.

used to unlock	keys
dollars and cents	money
opposite of no	yes
before two	one
comes from fire	smoke

Each monkey at the zoo eats 6 bananas every day. There are 7 monkeys. How many bananas will be needed for...

1 day?	42
2 days?	84
4 days?	168
1 week?	294

Write this sentence correctly.

Matt saw 7 monkies at the zoo.

Matt saw 7 monkeys at the zoo.

© Evan-Moor Corp. • EMC 3253 • Skill Sharpeners: Critical Thinking — Animals 9

Page 10

Think About It

How are monkeys the same as humans? How are they different? Fill in the chart with 3 ways for each.

Same	Different
Answers will vary.	

Jane went to Africa to see monkeys. She saw 3 fewer monkeys on the second day than she did on the first day. She saw 6 monkeys on the third day. She saw twice as many monkeys on the first day as she did on the third day. How many monkeys did Jane see on each day? How many did she see in all?

First day: __12__

Second day: __9__

Third day: __6__

In all: __27__

What is this?

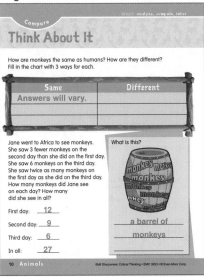

a barrel of

monkeys

10 Animals — Skill Sharpeners: Critical Thinking • EMC 3253 • © Evan-Moor Corp.

Page 11

Animal Idioms

Fill in the blank with the name of an animal from the box to complete each idiom.

Word Box

fly	ants
bat	goose
cat	bird
horse	camel
frog	monkeys
worms	mouse

1. _____ants_____ in your pants
2. _____frog_____ in my throat
3. as blind as a _____bat_____
4. Has the _____cat_____ got your tongue?
5. wouldn't hurt a _____fly_____
6. so hungry, I could eat a _____horse_____
7. more fun than a barrel of _____monkeys_____
8. as quiet as a _____mouse_____
9. a can of _____worms_____
10. a _____bird_____'s-eye view
11. go on a wild _____goose_____ chase
12. the straw that broke the _____camel_____'s back

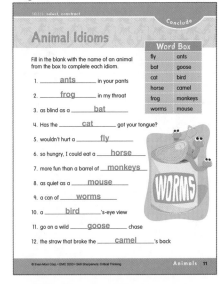

© Evan-Moor Corp. • EMC 3253 • Skill Sharpeners: Critical Thinking — Animals 11

Page 12

Word Problems

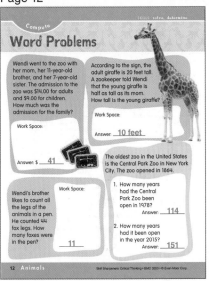

Wendi went to the zoo with her mom, her 11-year-old brother, and her 7-year-old sister. The admission to the zoo was $14.00 for adults and $9.00 for children. How much was the admission for the family?

Work Space:

Answer: $ __41__

According to the sign, the adult giraffe is 20 feet tall. A zookeeper told Wendi that the young giraffe is half as tall as its mom. How tall is the young giraffe?

Work Space:

Answer: __10 feet__

The oldest zoo in the United States is the Central Park Zoo in New York City. The zoo opened in 1864.

1. How many years had the Central Park Zoo been open in 1978? Answer: __114__

2. How many years had it been open in the year 2015? Answer: __151__

Wendi's brother likes to count all the legs of the animals in a pen. He counted 44 fox legs. How many foxes were in the pen?

Work Space:

__11__

12 Animals — Skill Sharpeners: Critical Thinking • EMC 3253 • © Evan-Moor Corp.

Page 13

Make a Monkey

Follow the directions to draw a monkey. Then color your monkey and fill in the blanks.

This monkey lives in the __Answers will vary.__

It uses its _____ and _____ to move in trees.

A monkey can _____

© Evan-Moor Corp. • EMC 3253 • Skill Sharpeners: Critical Thinking — Animals 13

Page 14

Monkey Words

Monkey begins with **MON**. Each of the answers to the clues also contains **MON**. Use the clues to complete the words. If a letter has a number below it, write that letter at the bottom of the page to find the kind of monkey that you see.

expensive gem	d i a MON d
popular board game	MON o p o l y
rare or unusual	u n c o m MON
scary creature	MON s t e r
12 in a year	MON t h s
type of nut	a l MON d
Japanese robe	k i MON o
coins and bills	MON e y
yellow fruit	l e MON

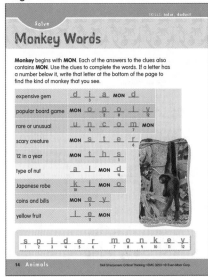

s p i d e r   m o n k e y
1 2 3 4 5 6   7 8 9 10 11 12

14 Animals — Skill Sharpeners: Critical Thinking • EMC 3253 • © Evan-Moor Corp.

Page 15

Monkey Snack

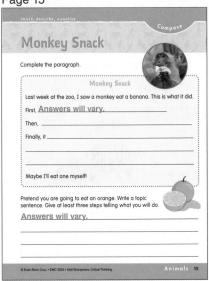

Complete the paragraph.

Monkey Snack

Last week at the zoo, I saw a monkey eat a banana. This is what it did.

First, **Answers will vary.**

Then, _____

Finally, it _____

Maybe I'll eat one myself!

Pretend you are going to eat an orange. Write a topic sentence. Give at least three steps telling what you will do.

Answers will vary.

© Evan-Moor Corp. • EMC 3253 • Skill Sharpeners: Critical Thinking — Animals 15

Page 16

Word Chains

To make a word chain, each word must begin with the same letter that the last word ends with. Finish the word chain for each category.

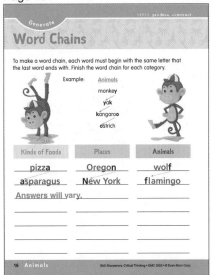

Example: _Animals_

monkey

yak

kangaroo

ostrich

Kinds of Foods	Places	Animals
pizza	Oregon	wolf
asparagus	New York	flamingo
Answers will vary.		

16 Animals — Skill Sharpeners: Critical Thinking • EMC 3253 • © Evan-Moor Corp.

Page 17

It's Feeding Time!

Tyson enjoys watching the zookeepers feed the animals. The feeding schedule for some of the zoo animals is given below. Design a schedule for Tyson so that he can see as many animals being fed as possible.

Remember:
- He wants to see each animal being fed for the full time.
- He can <u>not</u> see more than one animal at a time.

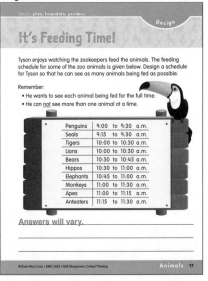

Penguins	9:00	to	9:30 a.m.
Seals	9:15	to	9:30 a.m.
Tigers	10:00	to	10:30 a.m.
Lions	10:00	to	10:30 a.m.
Bears	10:30	to	10:45 a.m.
Hippos	10:30	to	11:00 a.m.
Elephants	10:45	to	11:00 a.m.
Monkeys	11:00	to	11:30 a.m.
Apes	11:00	to	11:15 a.m.
Anteaters	11:15	to	11:30 a.m.

Answers will vary.

© Evan-Moor Corp. • EMC 3253 • Skill Sharpeners: Critical Thinking — Animals 17

Page 25

Tell What You Know

Bees

Do you like to have bees around? Explain why or why not.
<u>Answers will vary.</u>

Write three things you might see if you were a bee flying around.
1. <u>Answers will vary.</u>
2. _____
3. _____

Draw a bee busy at work.

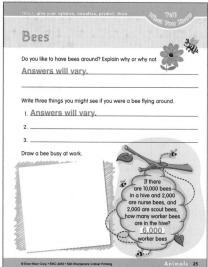

If there are 10,000 bees in a hive and 2,000 are nurse bees, and 2,000 are scout bees, how many worker bees are in the hive?
<u>6,000</u> worker bees

© Evan-Moor Corp. • EMC 3253 • Skill Sharpeners: Critical Thinking   Animals   25

Page 26

Bzzzzzzzz

Bee is to **hive** as **bird** is to _<u>nest</u>_
Bee is to **sting** as **mosquito** is to _<u>bite</u>_
Bee is to **yellow** as **polar bear** is to _<u>white</u>_

Bees can sting. What are 3 other animals that can sting?
<u>Answers will vary.</u>
1. _____ 2. _____ 3. _____

Bees have stripes. What are 3 other animals that have stripes?
1. _____ 2. _____ 3. _____

Betty Bee is an odd bee. She will gather nectar <u>only</u> from the flowers with odd-numbered products. Color those flowers.

4 x 5   6 x 4   7 x 5   6 x 8   3 x 8
7 x 3   9 x 7   2 x 7   7 x 7   9 x 3

26   Animals   Skill Sharpeners: Critical Thinking • EMC 3253 • © Evan-Moor Corp.

Page 27

Why Not?

Circle the picture or word in each line that does <u>not</u> share the same attributes as others in the line.

1. bee (spider) fly wasp gnat
Why? <u>because the others are insects</u>

2. cake pie cookie donut (pretzel)
Why? <u>because the others are sweet</u>

3. [shapes]
Why? <u>because the others have white space filled in</u>

4. daffodil tulip daisy (pine) rose
Why? <u>because the others are flowers</u>

5. [shapes]
Why? <u>because the others have lines around them</u>

© Evan-Moor Corp. • EMC 3253 • Skill Sharpeners: Critical Thinking   Animals   27

Page 28

Word Problems

Minna loves stuffed animals. Bees are her favorite. She displays her stuffed-animal collection in 2 cabinets. In one cabinet, there are 8 large animals on each shelf. In the other cabinet, there are 9 small animals on each shelf. If each cabinet has 7 shelves, how many large and small animals are in each cabinet? How many animals are in both cabinets?

Work Space:
<u>56</u> large animals
<u>63</u> small animals
<u>119</u> animals in all

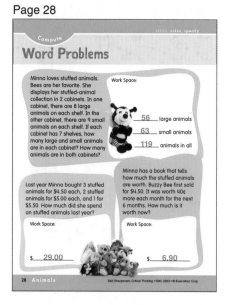

Last year Minna bought 3 stuffed animals for $4.50 each, 2 stuffed animals for $5.00 each, and 1 for $5.50. How much did she spend on stuffed animals last year?
Work Space:
$ <u>29.00</u>

Minna has a book that tells how much the stuffed animals are worth. Buzzy Bee first sold for $4.50. It was worth 40¢ more each month for the next 6 months. How much is it worth now?
Work Space:
$ <u>6.90</u>

28   Animals   Skill Sharpeners: Critical Thinking • EMC 3253 • © Evan-Moor Corp.

Page 29

Be Ready!

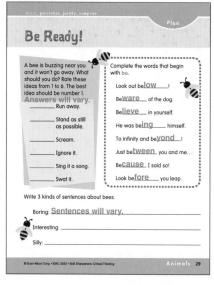

A bee is buzzing near you and it won't go away. What should you do? Rate these ideas from 1 to 6. The best idea should be number 1.
<u>Answers will vary.</u>
_____ Run away.
_____ Stand as still as possible.
_____ Scream.
_____ Ignore it.
_____ Sing it a song.
_____ Swat it.

Complete the words that begin with be.
Look out bel<u>ow</u> !
Be<u>ware</u> of the dog.
Bel<u>ieve</u> in yourself.
He was be<u>ing</u> himself.
To infinity and be<u>yond</u> !
Just be<u>tween</u> you and me…
Be<u>cause</u> I said so!
Look be<u>fore</u> you leap.

Write 3 kinds of sentences about bees.
Boring: <u>Sentences will vary.</u>
Interesting: _____
Silly: _____

© Evan-Moor Corp. • EMC 3253 • Skill Sharpeners: Critical Thinking   Animals   29

Page 30

It's a Bee!

Read about the parts of a worker bee.

- Her long tongue works like a straw. She uses it to sip nectar from flowers.
- She feels and smells with two antennae on her head.
- She has four wings that are used for flying.
- She crawls and climbs about on her six legs.
- She has three body parts—a head in front, a thorax in the middle, and an abdomen in back.
- She uses a stinger at the end of her abdomen to defend herself.

Label the parts of this bee.

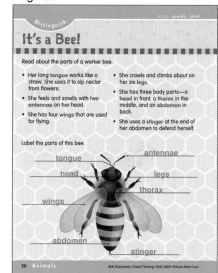

tongue   antennae
head   legs
   thorax
wings
abdomen
   stinger

30   Animals   Skill Sharpeners: Critical Thinking • EMC 3253 • © Evan-Moor Corp.

Page 31

A New Insect

You just discovered a new kind of insect! Answer the questions about your insect. Then draw a picture of your insect on the leaf.

1. What is your insect's name?
<u>Answers will vary.</u>

2. What size and shape is your insect?

3. What color is your insect?

4. Where does your insect live?

5. How does your insect get around?

6. What is special about your insect?

© Evan-Moor Corp. • EMC 3253 • Skill Sharpeners: Critical Thinking   Animals   31

Page 33

What's Important?

In each situation below, decide which details are relevant. Circle **all** the relevant details for each situation.
<u>Answers will vary.</u>

1. You are near a beehive.
- what you are eating
- if you disturb the hive
- if it is windy
- what you are wearing
- what you are drinking

2. You are making a cake.
- the temperature of the oven
- who likes cake
- what ingredients you need
- how long the cake needs to bake
- who gets the first piece

3. You are having a test in social studies.
- what the test is about
- the number of questions on the test
- what type of test it will be
- your score on the last test
- when the test is scheduled

Now try these on your own.

4. What details are **relevant** to buying your mother a birthday present?

5. What details are **irrelevant** to choosing a best friend?

© Evan-Moor Corp. • EMC 3253 • Skill Sharpeners: Critical Thinking   Animals   33

Page 34

A Honeybee's Body

Write the name of each body part of the honeybee's body on the correct line.

Word Box
antenna   leg   head   eye
pollen basket   tongue   stinger   wing

① antenna   ② eye   ③ head
④ wing
⑤ tongue
⑥ pollen basket   ⑦ leg
⑧ stinger

34   Animals   Skill Sharpeners: Critical Thinking • EMC 3253 • © Evan-Moor Corp.

---

136   Answer Key

Page 35

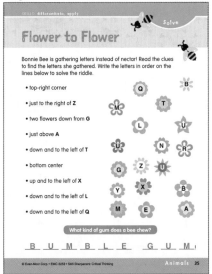

SKILLS: differentiate, apply

Solve

Flower to Flower

Bonnie Bee is gathering letters instead of nectar! Read the clues to find the letters she gathered. Write the letters in order on the lines below to solve the riddle.

- top-right corner
- just to the right of **Z**
- two flowers down from **G**
- just above **A**
- down and to the left of **T**
- bottom center
- up and to the left of **X**
- down and to the left of **L**
- down and to the left of **Q**

What kind of gum does a bee chew?

B U M B L E G U M

© Evan-Moor Corp. • EMC 3253 • Skill Sharpeners: Critical Thinking — Animals 35

Page 41

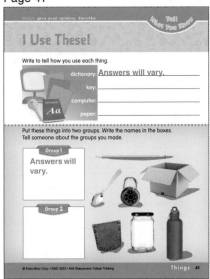

SKILLS: give your opinion, describe

Tell What You Know

I Use These!

Write to tell how you use each thing.

dictionary: **Answers will vary.**

key: ___

computer: ___

paper: ___

Put these things into two groups. Write the names in the boxes. Tell someone about the groups you made.

Group 1
Answers will vary.

Group 2

© Evan-Moor Corp. • EMC 3253 • Skill Sharpeners: Critical Thinking — Things 41

Page 42

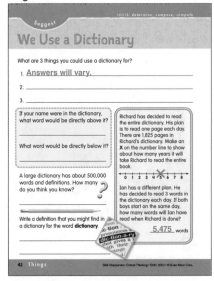

SKILLS: determine, compose, compute

Suggest

We Use a Dictionary

What are 3 things you could use a dictionary for?

1. **Answers will vary.**
2. ___
3. ___

If your name were in the dictionary, what word would be directly above it? ___

What word would be directly below it? ___

A large dictionary has about 500,000 words and definitions. How many do you think you know? ___

Write a definition that you might find in a dictionary for the word **dictionary**. ___

Richard has decided to read the entire dictionary. His plan is to read one page each day. There are 1,825 pages in Richard's dictionary. Make an **X** on the number line to show about how many years it will take Richard to read the entire book.

0 1 2 3 4 5 6 7 8

Ian has a different plan. He has decided to read 3 words in the dictionary each day. If both boys start on the same day, how many words will Ian have read when Richard is done?

5,475 words

42 Things — Skill Sharpeners: Critical Thinking • EMC 3253 • © Evan-Moor Corp.

Page 43

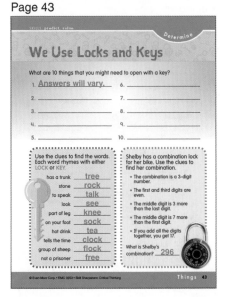

SKILLS: predict, solve

Determine

We Use Locks and Keys

What are 10 things that you might need to open with a key?

1. **Answers will vary.**   6. ___
2. ___   7. ___
3. ___   8. ___
4. ___   9. ___
5. ___   10. ___

Use the clues to find the words. Each word rhymes with either LOCK or KEY.

has a trunk — tree
stone — rock
to speak — talk
look — see
part of leg — knee
on your foot — sock
hot drink — tea
tells the time — clock
group of sheep — flock
not a prisoner — free

Shelby has a combination lock for her bike. Use the clues to find her combination.

- The combination is a 3-digit number.
- The first and third digits are even.
- The middle digit is 3 more than the last digit.
- The middle digit is 7 more than the first digit.
- If you add all the digits together, you get 17.

What is Shelby's combination? **296**

© Evan-Moor Corp. • EMC 3253 • Skill Sharpeners: Critical Thinking — Things 43

Page 44

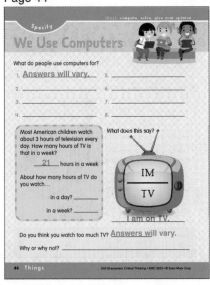

SKILLS: compute, solve, give your opinion

Specify

We Use Computers

What do people use computers for?

1. **Answers will vary.**   5. ___
2. ___   6. ___
3. ___   7. ___
4. ___   8. ___

Most American children watch about 3 hours of television every day. How many hours of TV is that in a week?

21 hours in a week

About how many hours of TV do you watch…

in a day? ___

in a week? ___

What does this say?

IM / TV

I am on TV

Do you think you watch too much TV? **Answers will vary.**

Why or why not? ___

44 Things — Skill Sharpeners: Critical Thinking • EMC 3253 • © Evan-Moor Corp.

Page 45

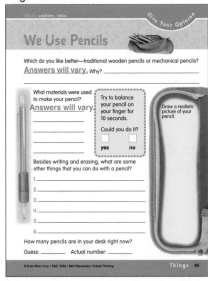

SKILLS: explain, infer

Give Your Opinion

We Use Pencils

Which do you like better—traditional wooden pencils or mechanical pencils? **Answers will vary.** Why? ___

What materials were used to make your pencil? **Answers will vary.** ___

Try to balance your pencil on your finger for 10 seconds. Could you do it?

yes   no

Draw a realistic picture of your pencil.

Besides writing and erasing, what are some other things that you can do with a pencil?

1. ___
2. ___
3. ___
4. ___
5. ___
6. ___

How many pencils are in your desk right now?

Guess: ___   Actual number: ___

© Evan-Moor Corp. • EMC 3253 • Skill Sharpeners: Critical Thinking — Things 45

Page 46

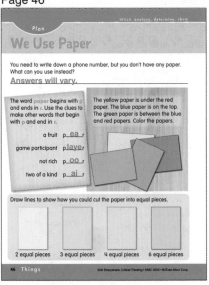

Plan

SKILLS: analyze, determine, show

We Use Paper

You need to write down a phone number, but you don't have any paper. What can you use instead?

Answers will vary.

The word *paper* begins with p and ends in r. Use the clues to make other words that begin with p and end in r.

a fruit — p ea r
game participant — p l ay er
not rich — p oo r
two of a kind — p ai r

The yellow paper is under the red paper. The blue paper is on the top. The green paper is between the blue and red papers. Color the papers.

Draw lines to show how you could cut the paper into equal pieces.

2 equal pieces   3 equal pieces   4 equal pieces   6 equal pieces

46 Things — Skill Sharpeners: Critical Thinking • EMC 3253 • © Evan-Moor Corp.

Page 47

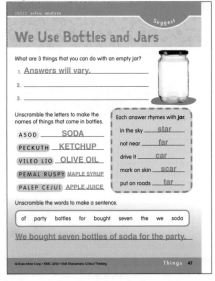

SKILLS: solve, analyze

Suggest

We Use Bottles and Jars

What are 3 things that you can do with an empty jar?

1. **Answers will vary.**
2. ___
3. ___

Unscramble the letters to make the names of things that come in bottles.

ASOD — **SODA**
PECKUTH — **KETCHUP**
VILEO LIO — **OLIVE OIL**
PEMAL RUSPY — **MAPLE SYRUP**
PALEP CEJUI — **APPLE JUICE**

Each answer rhymes with **jar**.

in the sky — star
not near — far
drive it — car
mark on skin — scar
put on roads — tar

Unscramble the words to make a sentence.

of party bottles for bought seven the we soda

We bought seven bottles of soda for the party.

© Evan-Moor Corp. • EMC 3253 • Skill Sharpeners: Critical Thinking — Things 47

Page 48

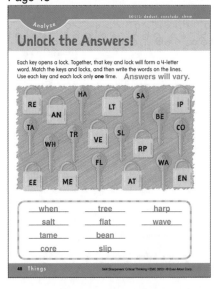

Analyze

SKILLS: deduct, conclude, show

Unlock the Answers!

Each key opens a lock. Together, that key and lock will form a 4-letter word. Match the keys and locks, and then write the words on the lines. Use each key and each lock only **one** time. **Answers will vary.**

HA   SA
RE   LT   IP
AN   BE
TA   TR   VE   SL   CO
WH   RP
FL   WA
EE   ME   AT   EN

when	tree	harp
salt	flat	wave
tame	bean	
core	slip	

48 Things — Skill Sharpeners: Critical Thinking • EMC 3253 • © Evan-Moor Corp.

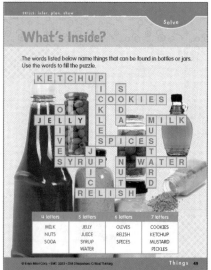

What's Inside?

The words listed below name things that can be found in bottles or jars. Use the words to fill the puzzle.

4 letters	5 letters	6 letters	7 letters
MILK	JELLY	OLIVES	COOKIES
NUTS	JUICE	RELISH	KETCHUP
SODA	SYRUP	SPICES	MUSTARD
	WATER		PICKLES

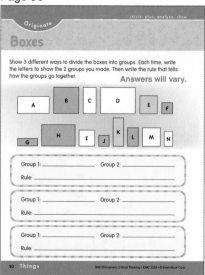

Boxes

Show 3 different ways to divide the boxes into groups. Each time, write the letters to show the 2 groups you made. Then write the rule that tells how the groups go together. **Answers will vary.**

Group 1: _____ Group 2: _____
Rule: _____

Group 1: _____ Group 2: _____
Rule: _____

Group 1: _____ Group 2: _____
Rule: _____

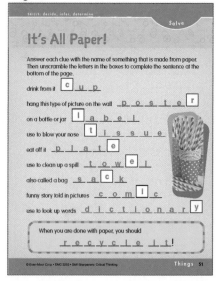

It's All Paper!

Answer each clue with the name of something that is made from paper. Then unscramble the letters in the boxes to complete the sentence at the bottom of the page.

drink from it — cup
hang this type of picture on the wall — poster
on a bottle or jar — label
use to blow your nose — tissue
eat off it — plate
use to clean up a spill — towel
also called a bag — sack
funny story told in pictures — comic
use to look up words — dictionary

When you are done with paper, you should recycle it!

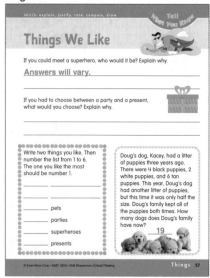

Things We Like

If you could meet a superhero, who would it be? Explain why.

Answers will vary.

If you had to choose between a party and a present, what would you choose? Explain why.

Write two things you like. Then number the list from 1 to 6. The one you like the most should be number 1.

_____ pets
_____ parties
_____ superheroes
_____ presents

Doug's dog, Kacey, had a litter of puppies three years ago. There were 4 black puppies, 2 white puppies, and 6 tan puppies. This year, Doug's dog had another litter of puppies, but this time it was only half the size. Doug's family kept all of the puppies both times. How many dogs does Doug's family have now?

19

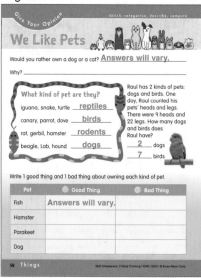

We Like Pets

Would you rather own a dog or a cat? **Answers will vary.**

Why? _____

What kind of pet are they?

iguana, snake, turtle — reptiles
canary, parrot, dove — birds
rat, gerbil, hamster — rodents
beagle, Lab, hound — dogs

Raul has 2 kinds of pets: dogs and birds. One day, Raul counted his pets' heads and legs. There were 9 heads and 22 legs. How many dogs and birds does Raul have?

2 dogs
7 birds

Write 1 good thing and 1 bad thing about owning each kind of pet.

Pet	😊 Good Thing	😞 Bad Thing
Fish	Answers will vary.	
Hamster		
Parakeet		
Dog		

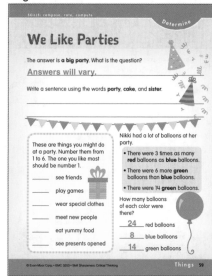

We Like Parties

The answer is a **big party**. What is the question?

Answers will vary.

Write a sentence using the words **party**, **cake**, and **sister**.

These are things you might do at a party. Number them from 1 to 6. The one you like most should be number 1.

_____ see friends
_____ play games
_____ wear special clothes
_____ meet new people
_____ eat yummy food
_____ see presents opened

Nikki had a lot of balloons at her party.
• There were 3 times as many **red** balloons as **blue** balloons.
• There were 6 more **green** balloons than **blue** balloons.
• There were 14 **green** balloons.

How many balloons of each color were there?

24 red balloons
8 blue balloons
14 green balloons

We Like Presents

What is the best present that you ever got? **Answers will vary.**
Why? _____
What is the best present that you ever gave?
Why? _____

You receive a present in a long, skinny box. What are 4 things that might be inside?

1. _____
2. _____
3. _____
4. _____

Janie made her mom a present. It took her 4 ½ hours to make it. She made the card, too. That took 45 minutes. It took 8 minutes to wrap the gift. Janie started her project at 10:15 in the morning. At what time did she finish?

3:38 pm

What do you think the expression "good things come in small packages" means? **good things come in small packages**

Size does not determine the value of something.

What are 3 good things that could come in small packages?

1. _____ 2. _____ 3. _____

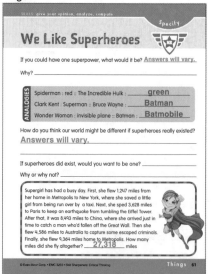

We Like Superheroes

If you could have one superpower, what would it be? **Answers will vary.**

Why? _____

ANALOGIES
Spiderman : red :: The Incredible Hulk : **green**
Clark Kent : Superman :: Bruce Wayne : **Batman**
Wonder Woman : invisible plane :: Batman : **Batmobile**

How do you think our world might be different if superheroes really existed?

Answers will vary.

If superheroes did exist, would you want to be one? _____
Why or why not? _____

Supergirl has had a busy day. First, she flew 1,247 miles from her home in Metropolis to New York, where she saved a little girl from being run over by a taxi. Next, she sped 3,628 miles to Paris to keep an earthquake from tumbling the Eiffel Tower. After that, it was 8,493 miles to China, where she arrived just in time to catch a man who'd fallen off the Great Wall. Then she flew 4,586 miles to Australia to capture some escaped criminals. Finally, she flew 9,364 miles home to Metropolis. How many miles did she fly altogether? **27,318** miles

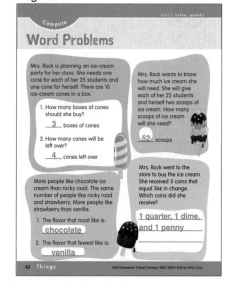

Word Problems

Mrs. Rock is planning an ice-cream party for her class. She needs one cone for each of her 25 students and one cone for herself. There are 10 ice-cream cones in a box.

Mrs. Rock wants to know how much ice cream she will need. She will give each of her 25 students and herself two scoops of ice cream. How many scoops of ice cream will she need?

52 scoops

1. How many boxes of cones should she buy?
3 boxes of cones

2. How many cones will be left over?
4 cones left over

More people like chocolate ice cream than rocky road. The same number of people like rocky road and strawberry. More people like strawberry than vanilla.

1. The flavor that most like is:
chocolate

2. The flavor that fewest like is:
vanilla

Mrs. Rock went to the store to buy the ice cream. She received 3 coins that equal 36¢ in change. Which coins did she receive?

1 quarter, 1 dime, and 1 penny

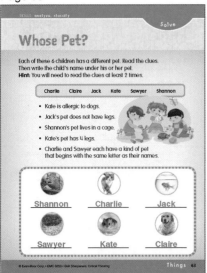

Page 63

SKILLS: analyze, classify

Solve

Whose Pet?

Each of these 6 children has a different pet. Read the clues.
Then write the child's name under his or her pet.
Hint: You will need to read the clues at least 2 times.

Charlie   Claire   Jack   Kate   Sawyer   Shannon

- Kate is allergic to dogs.
- Jack's pet does not have legs.
- Shannon's pet lives in a cage.
- Kate's pet has 4 legs.
- Charlie and Sawyer each have a kind of pet that begins with the same letter as their names.

Shannon   Charlie   Jack
Sawyer   Kate   Claire

Things 63

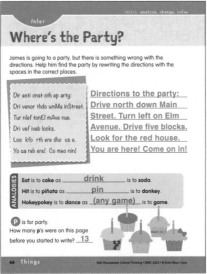

Page 64

Infer

SKILLS: analyze, change, solve

Where's the Party?

James is going to a party, but there is something wrong with the directions. Help him find the party by rewriting the directions with the spaces in the correct places.

Dir ecti onst oth ep arty:
Dri venor thdo wnMa inStreet.
Tur nlef tonEl mAve nue.
Dri vef iveb locks.
Loo kfo rth ere dho us e.
Yo ua reh ere! Co meo nin!

Directions to the party:
Drive north down Main
Street. Turn left on Elm
Avenue. Drive five blocks.
Look for the red house.
You are here! Come on in!

ANALOGIES

Eat is to cake as _drink_ is to soda.
Hit is to piñata as _pin_ is to donkey.
Hokeypokey is to dance as _(any game)_ is to game.

P is for party.
How many **p's** were on this page
before you started to write? _13_

64 Things

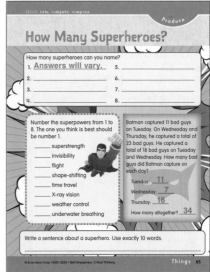

Page 65

SKILLS: rate, compute, compose

Produce

How Many Superheroes?

How many superheroes can you name?
1. **Answers will vary.**   5.
2.   6.
3.   7.
4.   8.

Number the superpowers from 1 to 8. The one you think is best should be number 1.
___ superstrength
___ invisibility
___ flight
___ shape-shifting
___ time travel
___ X-ray vision
___ weather control
___ underwater breathing

Batman captured 11 bad guys on Tuesday. On Wednesday and Thursday, he captured a total of 23 bad guys. He captured a total of 18 bad guys on Tuesday and Wednesday. How many bad guys did Batman capture on each day?

Tuesday: _11_
Wednesday: _7_
Thursday: _16_
How many altogether? _34_

Write a sentence about a superhero. Use exactly 10 words.

Things 65

Page 73

SKILLS: describe, compare

Tell What You Know

Family Tree

How many people are in your immediate family?

How many people are in your family, including grandparents, aunts, uncles, and cousins?

Answers will vary.
You are a son or a daughter. What other family roles do you have?

These 5 words describe my:
father
1.
2.
3.
4.
5.

How are you the same as your father?

How are you different from your father?

mother
1.
2.
3.
4.
5.

How are you the same as your mother?

How are you different from your mother?

Places 73

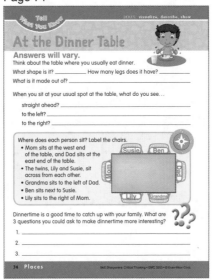

Page 74

Tell What You Know

SKILLS: visualize, describe, show

At the Dinner Table

Answers will vary.
Think about the table where you usually eat dinner.
What shape is it? _____ How many legs does it have? _____
What is it made out of? _____

When you sit at your usual spot at the table, what do you see…
straight ahead? _____
to the left? _____
to the right? _____

Where does each person sit? Label the chairs.
- Mom sits at the west end of the table, and Dad sits at the east end of the table.
- The twins, Lily and Susie, sit across from each other.
- Grandma sits to the left of Dad.
- Ben sits next to Susie.
- Lily sits to the right of Mom.

Susie   Ben
Mom   Dad
Lily   Grandma

Dinnertime is a good time to catch up with your family. What are 3 questions you could ask to make dinnertime more interesting?
1.
2.
3.

74 Places

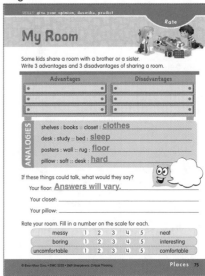

Page 75

SKILLS: give your opinion, describe, predict

Rate

My Room

Some kids share a room with a brother or a sister.
Write 3 advantages and 3 disadvantages of sharing a room.

Advantages	Disadvantages

ANALOGIES

shelves : books :: closet : _clothes_
desk : study :: bed : _sleep_
posters : wall :: rug : _floor_
pillow : soft :: desk : _hard_

If these things could talk, what would they say?
Your floor: **Answers will vary.**
Your closet:
Your pillow:

Rate your room. Fill in a number on the scale for each.

messy	1	2	3	4	5	neat
boring	1	2	3	4	5	interesting
uncomfortable	1	2	3	4	5	comfortable

Places 75

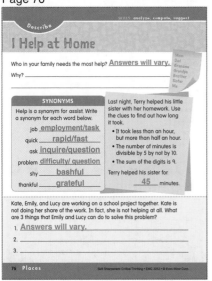

Page 76

Describe

I Help at Home

Who in your family needs the most help? **Answers will vary.**
Why?

SYNONYMS

Help is a synonym for assist. Write a synonym for each word below.
job _employment/task_
quick _rapid/fast_
ask _inquire/question_
problem _difficulty/ question_
shy _bashful_
thankful _grateful_

Last night, Terry helped his little sister with her homework. Use the clues to find out how long it took.
- It took less than an hour, but more than half an hour.
- The number of minutes is divisible by 5 by not by 10.
- The sum of the digits is 9.

Terry helped his sister for _45_ minutes.

Kate, Emily, and Lucy are working on a school project together. Kate is not doing her share of the work. In fact, she is not helping at all. What are 3 things that Emily and Lucy can do to solve this problem?
1. **Answers will vary.**
2.
3.

76 Places

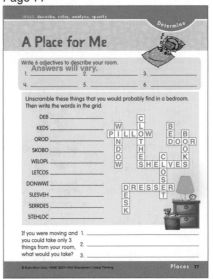

Page 77

SKILLS: describe, solve, analyze, specify

Determine

A Place for Me

Write 6 adjectives to describe your room.
Answers will vary.
1.   2.
3.   4.
5.   6.

Unscramble these things that you would probably find in a bedroom. Then write the words in the grid.

DEB _____
KEDS _____
OROD _____
SKOBO _____
WILOPL _____
LETCOS _____
DONWWI _____
SLESVEH _____
SERRDES _____
STEHLOC _____

W C
PILLOW
WINDOW
B
DOOR
BOOK
SHELVES
DRESSER
DESK

If you were moving and you could take only 3 things from your room, what would you take?
1.
2.
3.

Places 77

Page 78

Produce

Let's Eat!

It's Rainbow Week at the Smith house! During Rainbow Week, the family eats a different color meal each night. Each meal must contain a main dish, a side dish, a vegetable, and a beverage. Every item must be the correct color. Can you think of a menu for each night?

FARM FRESH

	Main Dish	Side Dish	Vegetable	Beverage
Monday yellow	Answers	will vary.		
Tuesday red				
Wednesday green				
Thursday brown				
Friday orange				
Saturday white				
Sunday purple				

Which night's dinner menu is your favorite? _____
Would you want to have Rainbow Week at your house? ○ YES ○ NO
Why or why not? _____

78 Places

Page 79

SKILLS: determine, infer, specify

Solve

Secret Number

Read the clues below to find the secret number. Each clue will help you eliminate one or more numbers. Cross out each number that you eliminate.

- This number is odd
- This number has 2 digits
- The digits of this number, added together, have a sum that is greater than 11.
- The digit 9 does not appear in this number.
- The first digit of this number is one greater than the second digit.

The secret number is __87__

© Evan-Moor Corp. • EMC 3253 • Skill Sharpeners: Critical Thinking   Places 79

Page 80

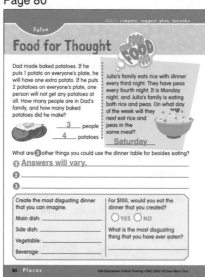

Solve

SKILLS: compute, suggest, plan, describe

Food for Thought

Dad made baked potatoes. If he puts 1 potato on everyone's plate, he will have one extra potato. If he puts 2 potatoes on everyone's plate, one person will not get any potatoes at all. How many people are in Dad's family, and how many baked potatoes did he make?

__3__ people
__4__ potatoes

Julia's family eats rice with dinner every third night. They have peas every fourth night. It is Monday night, and Julia's family is eating both rice and peas. On what day of the week will they next eat rice and peas in the same meal?
__Saturday__

What are 3 other things you could use the dinner table for besides eating?
① __Answers will vary.__
②
③

Create the most disgusting dinner that you can imagine.
Main dish:
Side dish:
Vegetable:
Beverage:

For $100, would you eat the dinner that you created?
○ YES ○ NO
What is the most disgusting thing that you have ever eaten?

80 Places   Skill Sharpeners: Critical Thinking • EMC 3253 • © Evan-Moor Corp.

Page 81

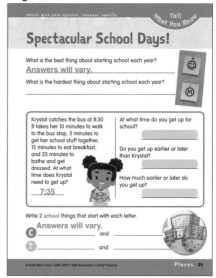

SKILLS: compare, analyze, explain

Categorize

My Family

Your grandmother's daughter is your
__mother or aunt__

Your father's grandfather is your
__great-grandfather__

Your mother's father is your
__grandfather__

Your grandfather's sister is your
__great aunt__

Your father's sister is your
__aunt__

Your sister's son would be your
__nephew__

Your uncle's child is your
__cousin__

Being the oldest or the youngest or an only child has advantages and disadvantages. Fill in the chart to show at least one for each.

	Advantages	Disadvantages
Oldest	Answers will vary.	
Youngest		
Only child		

If you could choose, would you want to be the oldest, the youngest, or an only child? _____ Why? _____

© Evan-Moor Corp. • EMC 3253 • Skill Sharpeners: Critical Thinking   Places 81

Page 82

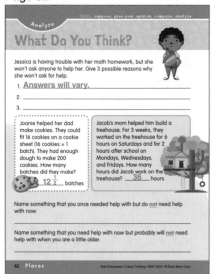

Analyze

SKILLS: suppose, give your opinion, compare, analyze

What Do You Think?

Jessica is having trouble with her math homework, but she won't ask anyone to help her. Give 3 possible reasons why she won't ask for help.

1. __Answers will vary.__
2.
3.

Joanie helped her dad make cookies. They could fit 16 cookies on a cookie sheet (16 cookies = 1 batch). They had enough dough to make 200 cookies. How many batches did they make?
__12½__ batches

Jacob's mom helped him build a treehouse. For 3 weeks, they worked on the treehouse for 6 hours on Saturdays and for 2 hours after school on Mondays, Wednesdays, and Fridays. How many hours did Jacob work on the treehouse? __36__ hours

Name something that you once needed help with but do not need help with now.

Name something that you need help with now but probably will not need help with when you are a little older.

82 Places   Skill Sharpeners: Critical Thinking • EMC 3253 • © Evan-Moor Corp.

Page 83

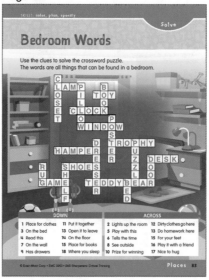

SKILLS: infer, plan, specify

Solve

Bedroom Words

Use the clues to solve the crossword puzzle. The words are all things that can be found in a bedroom.

CLAMP
CLOSET
TOY
CLOCK
WINDOW
HAMPER
TROPHY
SHOES
DESK
GAME
TEDDY BEAR

DOWN
1 Place for clothes
3 On the bed
4 Read this
7 On the wall
9 Has drawers
11 Put it together
13 Open it to leave
14 On the floor
15 Place for books
18 Where you sleep

ACROSS
2 Lights up the room
5 Play with this
6 Tells the time
8 See outside
10 Prize for winning
12 Dirty clothes go here
13 Do homework here
15 For your feet
16 Play it with a friend
17 Nice to hug

© Evan-Moor Corp. • EMC 3253 • Skill Sharpeners: Critical Thinking   Places 83

Page 89

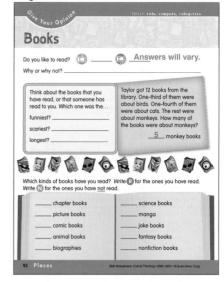

SKILLS: give your opinion, compute, specify

Tell What You Know

Spectacular School Days!

What is the best thing about starting school each year?
__Answers will vary.__

What is the hardest thing about starting school each year?

Krystal catches the bus at 8:30. It takes her 10 minutes to walk to the bus stop, 5 minutes to get her school stuff together, 15 minutes to eat breakfast, and 25 minutes to bathe and get dressed. At what time does Krystal need to get up?
__7:35__

At what time do you get up for school?

Do you get up earlier or later than Krystal?

How much earlier or later do you get up?

Write 2 school things that start with each letter.
__Answers will vary.__
C _____ and _____
T _____ and _____

© Evan-Moor Corp. • EMC 3253 • Skill Sharpeners: Critical Thinking   Places 89

Page 90

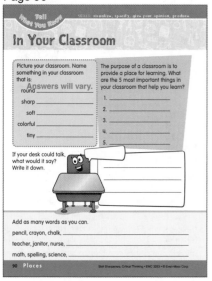

Tell What You Know

SKILLS: visualize, specify, give your opinion, produce

In Your Classroom

Picture your classroom. Name something in your classroom that is:
__Answers will vary.__
round
sharp
soft
colorful
tiny

The purpose of a classroom is to provide a place for learning. What are the 5 most important things in your classroom that help you learn?
1.
2.
3.
4.
5.

If your desk could talk, what would it say? Write it down.

Add as many words as you can.
pencil, crayon, chalk,
teacher, janitor, nurse,
math, spelling, science,

90 Places   Skill Sharpeners: Critical Thinking • EMC 3253 • © Evan-Moor Corp.

Page 91

SKILLS: analyze, change, specify

Solve

The First Day

Oh dear, it is only the first day of school, and Alex has already forgotten something important! For each clue, find the letter that is in the first boldfaced word but not in the second boldfaced word. Then write the letters in order on the lines at the bottom of this page to find out what Alex forgot.

- It is in CATCH but not in CACTUS.
- It is in KITE but not in TAKE.
- It is in CHEST but not in CHEAT.
- It is in SLIP but not in PIES.
- It is in PLUS but not in SLAP.
- It is in NICE but not in CITIES.
- It is in RICE but not in TIRES.
- It is in HARP but not in PARTY.

What can Alex do to solve his problem?
__Answers will vary.__

Alex forgot
__H I S__
__L U N C H__

© Evan-Moor Corp. • EMC 3253 • Skill Sharpeners: Critical Thinking   Places 91

Page 92

Give Your Opinion

SKILLS: rate, compute, categorize

Books

Do you like to read? _____ __Answers will vary.__
Why or why not?

Think about the books that you have read, or that someone has read to you. Which one was the…
funniest?
scariest?
longest?

Taylor got 12 books from the library. One-third of them were about birds. One-fourth of them were about cats. The rest were about monkeys. How many of the books were about monkeys?
__5__ monkey books

Which kinds of books have you read? Write R for the ones you have read. Write N for the ones you have not read.

___ chapter books	___ science books
___ picture books	___ manga
___ comic books	___ joke books
___ animal books	___ fantasy books
___ biographies	___ nonfiction books

92 Places   Skill Sharpeners: Critical Thinking • EMC 3253 • © Evan-Moor Corp.

Page 93

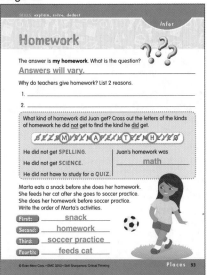

Homework

The answer is **my homework**. What is the question?
Answers will vary.

Why do teachers give homework? List 2 reasons.
1. _____
2. _____

What kind of homework did Juan get? Cross out the letters of the kinds of homework he did *not* get to find the kind he did get.

S P E L L I N G S C I E N C E Q U I Z

~~S~~ ~~P~~ ~~E~~ M ~~S~~ ~~P~~ ~~E~~ A ~~L~~ ~~L~~ T ~~I~~ ~~N~~ H ~~G~~ ~~S~~

He did not get SPELLING.
He did not get SCIENCE.
He did not have to study for a QUIZ.

Juan's homework was math

Marta eats a snack before she does her homework. She feeds her cat after she goes to soccer practice. She does her homework before soccer practice. Write the order of Marta's activities.

First: snack
Second: homework
Third: soccer practice
Fourth: feeds cat

Places 93

Page 94

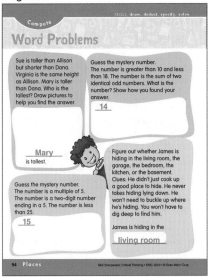

Word Problems

Sue is taller than Allison but shorter than Dana. Virginia is the same height as Allison. Mary is taller than Dana. Who is the tallest? Draw pictures to help you find the answer.

Mary
is tallest.

Guess the mystery number. The number is greater than 10 and less than 18. The number is the sum of two identical odd numbers. What is the number? Show how you found your answer.

14

Figure out whether James is hiding in the living room, the garage, the bedroom, the kitchen, or the basement. Clues: He didn't just cook up a good place to hide. He never takes hiding lying down. He won't need to buckle up where he's hiding. You won't have to dig deep to find him.

James is hiding in the
living room

Guess the mystery number. The number is a multiple of 5. The number is a two-digit number ending in a 5. The number is less than 25.

15

94 Places

Page 95

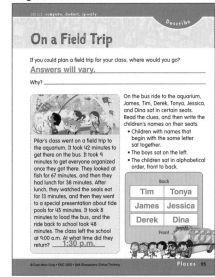

On a Field Trip

If you could plan a field trip for your class, where would you go?
Answers will vary.

Why?

On the bus ride to the aquarium, James, Tim, Derek, Tonya, Jessica, and Dina sat in certain seats. Read the clues, and then write the children's names on their seats.
• Children with names that begin with the same letter sat together.
• The boys sat on the left.
• The children sat in alphabetical order, front to back.

Pilar's class went on a field trip to the aquarium. It took 42 minutes to get there on the bus. It took 9 minutes to get everyone organized once they got there. They looked at fish for 67 minutes, and then they had lunch for 38 minutes. After lunch, they watched the seals eat for 13 minutes, and then they went to a special presentation about tide pools for 45 minutes. It took 8 minutes to load the bus, and the ride back to school took 48 minutes. The class left the school at 9:00 a.m. At what time did they return? 1:30 p.m.

Back
Tim	Tonya
James	Jessica
Derek	Dina
Front

Places 95

Page 96

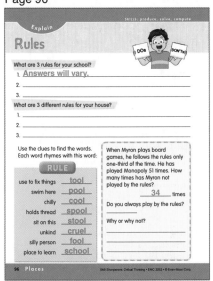

Rules

What are 3 rules for your school?
1. Answers will vary.
2. _____
3. _____

What are 3 different rules for your house?
1. _____
2. _____
3. _____

Use the clues to find the words. Each word rhymes with this word:

RULE

use to fix things — tool
swim here — pool
chilly — cool
holds thread — spool
sit on this — stool
unkind — cruel
silly person — fool
place to learn — school

When Myron plays board games, he follows the rules only one-third of the time. He has played Monopoly 51 times. How many times has Myron not played by the rules?
34 times

Do you always play by the rules?
Why or why not?

96 Places

Page 97

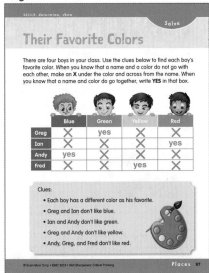

Their Favorite Colors

There are four boys in your class. Use the clues below to find each boy's favorite color. When you know that a name and a color do not go with each other, make an X under the color and across from the name. When you know that a name and color do go together, write **YES** in that box.

	Blue	Green	Yellow	Red
Greg	X	yes	X	X
Ian	X	X	X	yes
Andy	yes	X	X	X
Fred	X	X	yes	X

Clues:
• Each boy has a different color as his favorite.
• Greg and Ian don't like blue.
• Ian and Andy don't like green.
• Greg and Andy don't like yellow.
• Andy, Greg, and Fred don't like red.

Places 97

Page 98

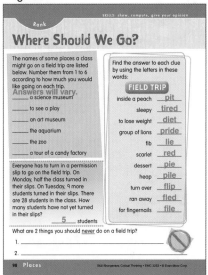

Where Should We Go?

The names of some places a class might go on a field trip are listed below. Number them from 1 to 6 according to how much you would like going on each trip.
Answers will vary.
____ a science museum
____ to see a play
____ an art museum
____ the aquarium
____ the zoo
____ a tour of a candy factory

Everyone has to turn in a permission slip to go on the field trip. On Monday, half the class turned in their slips. On Tuesday, 9 more students turned in their slips. There are 28 students in the class. How many students have not yet turned in their slips? 5 students

What are 2 things you should *never* do on a field trip?
1. _____
2. _____

Find the answer to each clue by using the letters in these words:

FIELD TRIP

inside a peach — pit
sleepy — tired
to lose weight — diet
group of lions — pride
fib — lie
scarlet — red
dessert — pie
heap — pile
turn over — flip
ran away — fled
for fingernails — file

98 Places

Page 99

Help!

Answers will vary. One possible path is shown.
Ryan has gotten separated from his class on the field trip. He needs to make it back to the bus before it leaves.

To help Ryan get back to the bus, start at the square in the upper-left corner. Move the same number of squares as the number shown (2). Move in a straight line in any direction. After you move two squares, move the same number of squares as the number shown in the box you are on.

Can you make a path that will take Ryan to the bus? Color the path.

2	7	3	6	1	7	2	1	8	4	3
3	2	2	6	3	1	3	7	5	2	9	1
1	2	5	1	2	8	1	2	2	6	6	2
1	3	4	2	7	2	4	1	7	1	1	7
2	7	3	6	1	3	4	9	1	8	4	3
1	3	4	2	7	2	4	2	7	2	1	7
5	2	2	6	3	1	3	7	5	2	9	1
7	8	1	6	2	4	3	6	4	2	6	2
2	7	3	6	1	4	9	2	1	1	4	6
1	3	4	2	7	2	3	8	3	7	2	1
7	8	1	6	2	1	1	4	2	6	1	3
5	2	2	8	1	3	1	3	5	3	4	9

Places 99

Page 105

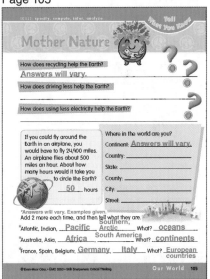

Mother Nature

How does recycling help the Earth?
Answers will vary.

How does driving less help the Earth?

How does using less electricity help the Earth?

If you could fly around the Earth in an airplane, you would have to fly 24,900 miles. An airplane flies about 500 miles an hour. About how many hours would it take you to circle the Earth?
50 hours

Where in the world are you?
Continent: Answers will vary.
Country: _____
State: _____
County: _____
City: _____
Street: _____

*Answers will vary. Examples given.
Add 2 more each time, and then tell what they are.

*Atlantic, Indian, Pacific, Arctic, Southern. What? oceans

*Australia, Asia, Africa, South America. What? continents

*France, Spain, Belgium, Germany, Italy. What? European countries

Our World 105

Page 106

Reuse and Recycle

When we reuse things instead of throwing them away, we save resources and we don't fill up landfills. How could you reuse each of these items?
soda bottle Answers will vary.
egg carton _____
old magazines _____
torn shirt _____

SYNONYMS
Garbage is a synonym for trash. Write a synonym for each below.
bin — container/receptacle
smelly — stinky
slimy — gooey
broken — ruined/shattered
soiled — dirty
disgusting — gross/revolting

Mr. Smith takes out his garbage on Mondays and Thursdays. Mr. Jones takes out his garbage once every 3 days. Both men have taken out their garbage today. Today is Thursday, March 6. On what date will both men take out their garbage on the same day again? Monday, March 24

Fill in the can that shows what percentage of waste you think your family recycles weekly.
50% 33% 25% 20%

106 Our World

Page 107

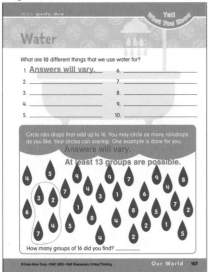

Water

SKILLS: specify, show — Tell What You Know

What are 10 different things that we use water for?

1. Answers will vary.   6. _____
2. _____   7. _____
3. _____   8. _____
4. _____   9. _____
5. _____   10. _____

Circle rain drops that add up to 16. You may circle as many raindrops as you like. Your circles can overlap. One example is done for you.

Answers will vary.
At least 13 groups are possible.

How many groups of 16 did you find? _____

Page 108

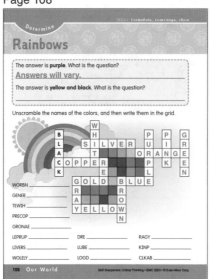

Rainbows

Determine — SKILLS: formulate, rearrange, show

The answer is **purple**. What is the question?
Answers will vary.

The answer is **yellow and black**. What is the question?

Unscramble the names of the colors, and then write them in the grid.

WORBN _____   GENER _____   TEWIH _____   PRECOP _____   GRONAE _____
LEPRUP _____   DRE _____   RAGY _____
LIVERS _____   LUBE _____   KINP _____
WOLELY _____   LOGD _____   CLKAB _____

Grid answers: BLACK, WHITE, SILVER, PURPLE, PING, GREEN, COPPER, ORANGE, GOLD, BLUE, BROWN, YELLOW

Page 109

The Night Sky

SKILLS: compare, specify — Analyze

How many stars are in the shapes?

triangle only __7__   triangle and circle __9__
rectangle only __7__   triangle and rectangle __8__
circle only __6__   all three shapes total __35__
circle and rectangle __8__   no shapes __7__

Page 110

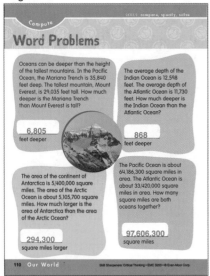

Word Problems

Compute — SKILLS: compare, specify, solve

Oceans can be deeper than the height of the tallest mountains. In the Pacific Ocean, the Mariana Trench is 35,840 feet deep. The tallest mountain, Mount Everest, is 29,035 feet tall. How much deeper is the Mariana Trench than Mount Everest is tall?

__6,805__ feet deeper

The average depth of the Indian Ocean is 12,598 feet. The average depth of the Atlantic Ocean is 11,730 feet. How much deeper is the Indian Ocean than the Atlantic Ocean?

__868__ feet deeper

The area of the continent of Antarctica is 5,400,000 square miles. The area of the Arctic Ocean is about 5,105,700 square miles. How much larger is the area of Antarctica than the area of the Arctic Ocean?

__294,300__ square miles larger

The Pacific Ocean is about 64,186,300 square miles in area. The Atlantic Ocean is about 33,420,000 square miles in area. How many square miles are both oceans together?

__97,606,300__ square miles

Page 111

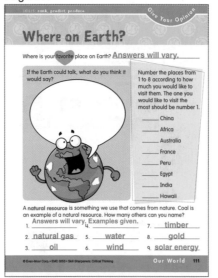

Where on Earth?

SKILLS: rank, predict, produce — Give Your Opinion

Where is your favorite place on Earth? Answers will vary.

If the Earth could talk, what do you think it would say?

Number the places from 1 to 8 according to how much you would like to visit them. The one you would like to visit the most should be number 1.

_____ China
_____ Africa
_____ Australia
_____ France
_____ Peru
_____ Egypt
_____ India
_____ Hawaii

A natural resource is something we use that comes from nature. Coal is an example of a natural resource. How many others can you name?

Answers will vary. Examples given.

1. _____   4. _____   7. __timber__
2. __natural gas__   5. __water__   8. __gold__
3. __oil__   6. __wind__   9. __solar energy__

Page 112

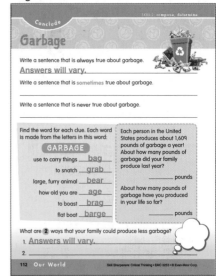

Garbage

Conclude — SKILLS: compare, determine

Write a sentence that is **always** true about garbage.
Answers will vary.

Write a sentence that is **sometimes** true about garbage.
_____

Write a sentence that is **never** true about garbage.
_____

Find the word for each clue. Each word is made from the letters in this word:

GARBAGE

use to carry things __bag__
to snatch __grab__
large, furry animal __bear__
how old you are __age__
to boast __brag__
flat boat __barge__

Each person in the United States produces about 1,609 pounds of garbage a year! About how many pounds of garbage did your family produce last year?
_____ pounds

About how many pounds of garbage have you produced in your life so far?
_____ pounds

What are **2** ways that your family could produce less garbage?
1. Answers will vary.
2. _____

Page 113

All Wet

SKILLS: analyze, generate — Produce

The word **rain** contains the letters **r** and **n**. How many other words can you make that contain both of these letters? The **r** must come before the **n**. *Examples:* run, grant

1. Answers will vary.   6. _____   11. _____
2. _____   7. _____   12. _____
3. _____   8. _____   13. _____
4. _____   9. _____   14. _____
5. _____   10. _____   15. _____

The word **wet** contains the letters **w** and **t**. See how many other words you can make that contain **w** and **t**. The **w** must come before the **t**.

1. _____   6. _____   11. _____
2. _____   7. _____   12. _____
3. _____   8. _____   13. _____
4. _____   9. _____   14. _____
5. _____   10. _____   15. _____

Page 114

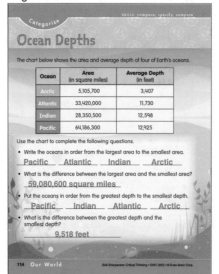

Ocean Depths

Categorize — SKILLS: compare, specify, compute

The chart below shows the area and average depth of four of Earth's oceans.

Ocean	Area (in square miles)	Average Depth (in feet)
Arctic	5,105,700	3,407
Atlantic	33,420,000	11,730
Indian	28,350,500	12,598
Pacific	64,186,300	12,925

Use the chart to complete the following questions.

• Write the oceans in order from the largest area to the smallest area.
__Pacific__ __Atlantic__ __Indian__ __Arctic__

• What is the difference between the largest area and the smallest area?
__59,080,600 square miles__

• Put the oceans in order from the greatest depth to the smallest depth.
__Pacific__ __Indian__ __Atlantic__ __Arctic__

• What is the difference between the greatest depth and the smallest depth?
__9,518 feet__

Page 115

What's in the Can?

SKILLS: analyze, describe, conclude — Infer

Some archaeologists study the garbage of ancient cultures to learn about how people lived. What can you learn about the Smith family by studying their garbage? Write about it below.

What are 3 things that you *know* about this family?
1. Answers will vary.
2. _____
3. _____

What are 3 things that are *probably* true about this family?
1. _____
2. _____
3. _____

What are 3 things that *might* be true about this family?
1. _____
2. _____
3. _____

Found in the Smith Family's Garbage and Recycling
• rice cakes bag
• diet soda bottle
• wilted lettuce leaves
• carrot peelings
• tomato stems
• broken mousetrap
• chocolate cake mix box
• frosting container
• 10 half-burned candles
• crumpled wrapping paper
• ice-cream carton
• school lunch calendar
• town pool schedule
• sugarless gum wrappers
• dead flowers
• *American Girl* magazine
• *Boys' Life* magazine
• 3 dog food cans
• large pizza box
• lice shampoo bottle
• nonfat yogurt container
• allergy pill bottle
• microwave popcorn bag
• broken Beatles CD
• veggie burger box
• hamburger bun bag
• onion skins
• 2 lottery tickets
• unidentifiable moldy stuff

Page 117

Earth Day

Find

Find the words hidden in the puzzle.

```
C L E A N A N I M A L S R
A C A R E E X T I N C T W
R I N E W N A Q L M P T O
E X R U A E M R I C E E R
C O N S E R V A T I O N L
Y X F S E G S P I H P O D
L G S S E 2 I M R X E O A
E E A P O L L U T I O N T
E N V I R O N M E N T E E
S E E V O L U N T E E R R
E C U D E R N O W P L E H
```

air	Earth	litter	recycle	volunteer
animals	energy	oxygen	reduce	water
care	environment	ozone	reuse	world
clean	extinct	people	save	
conservation	fuel	pollution	soil	

© Evan-Moor Corp. • EMC 3253 • Skill Sharpeners: Critical Thinking

Our World 117

Page 121

Plants

Tell What You Know

Write three reasons that Earth needs plants.

1. **Answers will vary.**
2. _____
3. _____

What kinds of plants are most important to you? Explain why.

Olisa has a garden shop. She has 54 snapdragon plants. One customer wants to buy 42 snapdragon plants. There are 6 snapdragons in a pack.

How many packs should Olisa sell to her customer?

___**7**___ packs

How many packs will Olisa have left?

___**2**___ packs

Draw to finish the pattern.

© Evan-Moor Corp. • EMC 3253 • Skill Sharpeners: Critical Thinking

Our World 121

Page 122

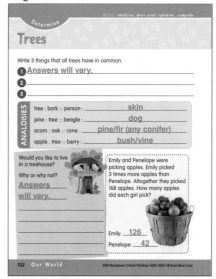

Trees

Determine

Write 3 things that all trees have in common.

1 **Answers will vary.**
2 _____
3 _____

ANALOGIES

tree : bark :: person : ___**skin**___
pine : tree :: beagle : ___**dog**___
acorn : oak :: cone : ___**pine/fir (any conifer)**___
apple : tree :: berry : ___**bush/vine**___

Would you like to live in a treehouse? Why or why not? **Answers will vary.**

Emily and Penelope were picking apples. Emily picked 3 times more apples than Penelope. Altogether they picked 168 apples. How many apples did each girl pick?

Emily: ___**126**___

Penelope: ___**42**___

122 Our World

Skill Sharpeners: Critical Thinking • EMC 3253 • © Evan-Moor Corp.

Page 123

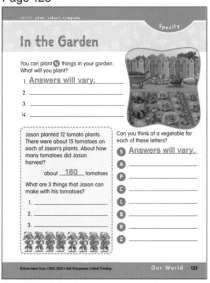

In the Garden

Specify

You can plant **4** things in your garden. What will you plant?

1. **Answers will vary.**
2. _____
3. _____
4. _____

Jason planted 12 tomato plants. There were about 15 tomatoes on each of Jason's plants. About how many tomatoes did Jason harvest?

about ___**180**___ tomatoes

What are 3 things that Jason can make with his tomatoes?

1. _____
2. _____
3. _____

Can you think of a vegetable for each of these letters?

Answers will vary.

S
A
P
C
L
B
R
Z

© Evan-Moor Corp. • EMC 3253 • Skill Sharpeners: Critical Thinking

Our World 123

Page 124

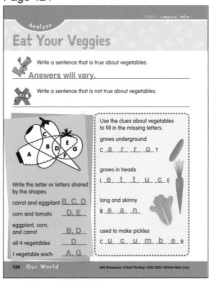

Eat Your Veggies

Analyze

Write a sentence that is true about vegetables.

Answers will vary.

Write a sentence that is not true about vegetables.

Write the letter or letters shared by the shapes.

carrot and eggplant ___**B, C, D**___
corn and tomato ___**D, E**___
eggplant, corn, and carrot ___**B, D**___
all 4 vegetables ___**D**___
1 vegetable each ___**A, G**___

Use the clues about vegetables to fill in the missing letters.

grows underground

c a r r o t

grows in heads

l e t t u c e

long and skinny

b e a n

used to make pickles

c u c u m b e r

124 Our World

Skill Sharpeners: Critical Thinking • EMC 3253 • © Evan-Moor Corp.

Page 125

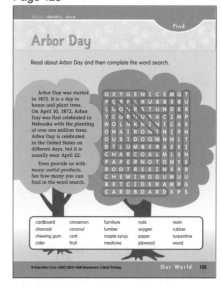

Arbor Day

Find

Read about Arbor Day and then complete the word search.

Arbor Day was started in 1872. It is a day to honor and plant trees. On April 10, 1872, Arbor Day was first celebrated in Nebraska with the planting of over one million trees. Arbor Day is celebrated in the United States on different days, but it is usually near April 22.

Trees provide us with many useful products. See how many you can find in the word search.

```
O X Y G E N I C E M Q T
P C B F L R U B B E R U
L O O R S T U N D E R R
Y C G R U U S A C I M P
W O L N K N I V I C A E
O N A I R O N T N I P N
O U S T D O O W N N L T
D T L U M B E R A E E I
C H A R C O A L M L S N
P A P E R N O T O M Y E
R O O T R E S I N S R B
C H E W I N G G U M U U
B X T C I D E R A M P G
C A R D B O A R D X P S
```

cardboard	cinnamon	furniture	nuts	resin
charcoal	coconut	lumber	oxygen	rubber
chewing gum	cork	maple syrup	paper	turpentine
cider	fruit	medicine	plywood	wood

© Evan-Moor Corp. • EMC 3253 • Skill Sharpeners: Critical Thinking

Our World 125

Page 126

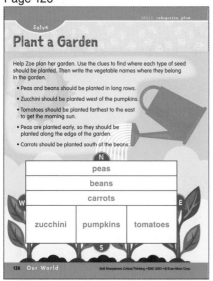

Plant a Garden

Solve

Help Zoe plan her garden. Use the clues to find where each type of seed should be planted. Then write the vegetable names where they belong in the garden.

- Peas and beans should be planted in long rows.
- Zucchini should be planted west of the pumpkins.
- Tomatoes should be planted farthest to the east to get the morning sun.
- Peas are planted early, so they should be planted along the edge of the garden.
- Carrots should be planted south of the beans.

N		
peas		
beans		
carrots		
zucchini	pumpkins	tomatoes

W ... E ... S

126 Our World

Skill Sharpeners: Critical Thinking • EMC 3253 • © Evan-Moor Corp.

Page 127

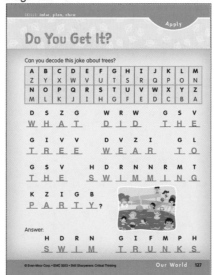

Do You Get It?

Apply

Can you decode this joke about trees?

A	B	C	D	E	F	G	H	I	J	K	L	M
Z	Y	X	W	V	U	T	S	R	Q	P	O	N
N	O	P	Q	R	S	T	U	V	W	X	Y	Z
M	L	K	J	I	H	G	F	E	D	C	B	A

D S Z G → **WHAT**
W R W → **DID**
G S V → **THE**

G I V V → **TREE**
D V Z I → **WEAR**
G L → **TO**

G S V → **THE**
H D R N N R M T → **SWIMMING**

K Z I G B → **PARTY**?

Answer:

H D R N → **SWIM**
G I F M P H → **TRUNKS**

© Evan-Moor Corp. • EMC 3253 • Skill Sharpeners: Critical Thinking

Our World 127

Page 128

About Trees

Solve

Use the clues to complete the crossword puzzle.

ARBOR DAY
BARK
CARBON DIOXIDE
CROWN
DECIDUOUS
EVERGREEN
LEAVES
LIMB
NUTS
OXYGEN
ROOTS

Across
1. the food-making part of a tree
3. trees that drop their leaves in the winter
7. the outer covering of a tree's trunk
9. trees absorb this, which helps clean the air
11. tree seeds that people eat

Down
2. a special day to celebrate trees
4. trees that remain green all year
5. another name for a tree branch
6. tree leaves release this into the air
8. the branches and leaves of a tree form a _____
10. these absorb water from the soil

128 Our World

Skill Sharpeners: Critical Thinking • EMC 3253 • © Evan-Moor Corp.

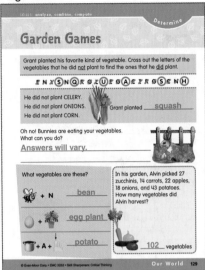

Garden Games

Grant planted his favorite kind of vegetable. Cross out the letters of the vegetables that he did not plant to find the ones that he did plant.

E X X S N Q R G L U F G A C F R G S C N H

He did not plant CELERY.
He did not plant ONIONS.
He did not plant CORN.

Grant planted ___squash___

Oh no! Bunnies are eating your vegetables.
What can you do?
__Answers will vary.__

What vegetables are these?

+ N ___bean___

+ ___egg plant___

+ A + ___potato___

In his garden, Alvin picked 27 zucchinis, 14 carrots, 22 apples, 18 onions, and 43 potatoes. How many vegetables did Alvin harvest?

___102___ vegetables

© Evan-Moor Corp. • EMC 3253 • Skill Sharpeners: Critical Thinking